MARGARET THE PERSON

Published by

Librario Publishing Ltd.

ISBN: 1-904440-52-5

Copies can be ordered via the Internet
www.librario.com

or from:

Brough House, Milton Brodie, Kinloss
Moray IV36 2UA
Tel/Fax No 00 44 (0)1343 850 617

Printed and bound by
DigiSource UK Ltd, Livingston

MARGARET THE PERSON

MARGARET HURDMAN

Librario

Margaret The Person

This is the story of my life and experiences gained, of thoughts and happenings that have prompted me to relate to others the wonders of working with Spirit.

My aim is to confirm what I was shown on a very special day in the springtime of 1970, the day I died during open-heart surgery; that was my new beginning, the day I was reborn to a different me. I was then thirty-two years old.

Thankfully I have the support of a close loving family – my husband John, our sons Stephen, Kenneth and Andrew, my daughters-in-law and wonderful grandchildren, and an added bonus of two great-granddaughters.

My husband is an honest man and has never denied me my thoughts. He has always supported me in the work that I do. I know that I am not an easy person to live with; I am a scatterbrain and that is enough to drive a saint mad. I seem to be often in a different dimension, and I live on a roundabout of life.

I was born in the Midlands town of Kidderminster, once very famous for its carpet factories. My childhood was a happy time as I had the love of very special parents, and a brother so different to me, physically and I think also mentally. He had the tall good looks; I am the short, rounded type.

I met my husband John when I was just turned sixteen and we married in the October following my eighteenth birthday in September. Life was not easy in those days and John worked all the hours he could; money was short.

We had been married 18 months when our first child arrived, but tragically he was stillborn. This was our first major trial of life and it was not easy to accept that our much-wanted baby had to go back to God. We were both devastated, but time passed and we had three other healthy sons.

Then came my biggest learning lesson when I died during heart surgery. In fact I entered the world of Spirit three times, an experience, which my life turned full circle and produced a new me. I had found my path.

The road is not easy, as any aspiring medium will tell you. My destiny was decided and I studied, as I still do, to obtain a greater knowledge. We moved to Llandudno in North Wales where I was to develop and progress along my path of spirituality. I was working for Spirit.

Many of the episodes are of happenings, which are recorded and are still occurring to me today. My work now takes me to churches, and similar groups, teaching others what I know. Personal contacts with readings have opened doors for me and during the last two years I have travelled to other countries giving evidence of survival after death.

This is the work I believe I was sent back to do, all those years ago. When I have completed the task that was meant of me, then I, like everyone else, will return back home to Spirit. I truly hope to be worthy of my second chance. I am very thankful to my Spirit friends and especially to earthly friends, since without their help life would not be so easy and I would have much difficulty in doing the work I do.

Perhaps you, my friend, can relate to some of my happenings and reminiscences but I feel that there is still more to tell.

Whatever path you tread, whatever way you walk, remember you are a child of God.

Margaret The Person

By Margaret Hurdman

I was born in September 1938 before the outbreak of World War II, and I was just twelve months old when my father was called up. This was the same pattern for many people and I did not see him again until I was almost five.

In those early years, dad was the man whose photograph stood on our mantelshelf and whose letters were eagerly awaited. Occasionally he sent us a small parcel; its contents becoming the centre of our universe for a few precious moments, for each parcel meant the world to us. Looking back to my childhood I think that even in those days I knew my dad was really special. He was simply a man who warmed my heart with his photo-smile.

One day a parcel arrived when he sent a penknife for my big brother Bob and a pair of socks for me. Inside one of the socks was a banana, the first one I had ever seen! I realise now that it must have been green when he sent it, but it arrived mouldy and squashed and to this day I shudder as I think of it! It was many years before anyone could convince me to go anywhere near another banana. In gingerly exploring the remaining sock, which seemed harmless enough, it soon became apparent that there was something inside it. But this time it felt hard and I squealed as my brother quickly volunteered that it was a snake. Not having a clue what a snake looked like, I was much relieved (and so was he, although he would never admit it), when it turned out to be a beautiful moonstone necklace for mum. I have the necklace today and it is one of my most treasured possessions. It is still as pretty as when it was sent to my mother all those years ago and the stones seem to be full of energy. I can always rely on it to raise my spirits and rejuvenate me when I wear it, perhaps because it represents love. It is certainly special.

On another occasion dad sent us two pillowcases, which he had embroidered with a picture of Donald Duck! Today it seems ridiculous to remember but imagine how strange a contrast it must have been, this man, my father, fighting in the Burma jungle and yet being capable of creating such lovely work. He was a gifted artist and I remember the likeness he captured when he copied a picture of us. I wish I knew what happened to those images, which disappeared sometime after he came home. Maybe he was dissatisfied with them and threw them away.

During those years when he was absent, money was in short supply. My mum worked day shifts in the local ammunition factory. The routine was that she would drop me at aunty Alice's house, deposit my brother at school and then she would clock on for work. "Literally clock on," she said. She told us how she used to put a card in a type of clock and 'punch' it to prove at what time she arrived and also when she left.

My brother hated school and resented every moment, so as soon as my mother was out of eyesight, he would be off, playing truant. He spent many hours in a nearby American Army camp, not far from where we actually lived, hanging around until school broke up for the day. He had a knack of sauntering home at the right time, so it never occurred to him that he would be found out. These things have a way of coming around which he found out, much to his cost!

One Saturday morning there was a knock at the door and there stood a man with a stern expression on his face. Yes, he was the truant officer. My mother stood there ready to explode. What was this man saying, her son Bob not going to school? In fact he had not been in school for three whole weeks! As the facts emerged so did the truth and my brother was given a strong punishment. My poor mum. What made her even angrier was that he had been wasting the food that he took for his school lunches. Apparently the Americans were feeding him and he was giving his food to the birds! Another lesson for my brother – beware the truant officer!

During the daytime aunt Alice, mum's sister, looked after me, as I was too young for school. Even in those days I always seemed to be ill. I had caught a very bad dose of measles, which had left me with problems in one eye. Measles was a serious disease at that time and many children died as a result of catching it. For me, this illness was a huge problem, medical care and knowledge being nowhere near as advanced as it is today. I lost the sight in my right eye, which then developed complications, and years of painful treatment followed.

When my mother first took me to aunt Alice's house I resented her. She seemed aloof and so 'posh' and everything seemed to smell of soap. Indeed her house was spotless and I had to behave myself – or else! I had no idea that she loved me though and it was years before I came to realise just how much

One day I really blotted my copybook. I loved to gaze into the china cabinet and even now I have no idea what actually happened, but somehow I managed to pull the cabinet on top of me. I escaped unscathed, just very scared. Aunty Alice's prized bits and pieces clattered down and I was sent to bed! She was very good about it but my first thought was to run away, the second was 'where to?' However, I was saved by my cousin Bill, who was auntie's only child, about ten years older than I was. He came to talk to me that night and I have to say that Roy Rogers was nothing compared to Bill, my hero!

My brother and I were lucky in many ways, for when we were at home in the evenings we were always warm and we all ate well, with the help (unofficially of course) of the American Camp. Bob's visits would produce sweets and cigarettes for my mum, not to mention tins of fruit, which were real treats for us.

Those same tins of fruit are etched on my mind. Bob had been given four tins of peaches and mum decided to keep them until Christmas. It was a week before Christmas when rations were making things tight for everyone. There was to be a tin each for Alice and gran. Mum had entered a raffle in the factory where she worked and all she would say was that there was something very special as the prize. On Christmas Eve, mum sent Bob down into the cellar where our goodies were stored to fetch the tins of peaches. He brought them upstairs and mum produced a tin opener, which was when the trouble started.

Unknown to my mother, my brother had already pierced the cans some time before and drunk the juice, so all the peaches were mouldy! My brother's backside ended up being rather red and hot and he was sent to bed on Christmas Eve feeling very sorry for himself and being told that there was no Father Christmas – to which he replied, "I don't believe in him anyway!" Sadly neither Alice nor gran received their tins of peaches. However, that night there was a knock on the door. It was a man with a parcel and it turned out that my mother had won a 5ft doll in the work's raffle. To my delight, on Christmas morning I found this wondrous gift from Santa. The clothes the doll wore were much too big for me and I was in heaven! My brother, now forgiven because it was Christmas, was happy with the gift of model planes and pencils. My mum was good like that; she always brought love back into our lives.

For Christmas lunch we went to gran and grandad's. Joy of joys, we had two roast rabbits and of course the trimmings AND Christmas pudding! A feast indeed but no one seemed to know the real source of the dinner. I understand that grandad had been out walking two nights before with a piece of string – we enquired no further and it was never spoken of again.

But that Christmas Day was so special, for Alice's husband, Sid, was home on leave. Uncle Sid only had a very short leave, so Alice was as happy as she could be during those two days. When the day came to see Sid off to war again, Alice asked my mother to go with her. In fact we all went, mum, Alice, Bob, Bill and I. We took the train to Hull in Yorkshire and what an adventure it was. The trains in those days had no corridors, which meant there were no toilets. Mum began to look very uncomfortable and quite obviously needed the lavatory, but the train did not stop before we reached Hull and mum was desperate. Alice, with a stroke of genius produced her rain hood as a makeshift loo much to mum's evident relief. But when she let down the leather strap to lower the window to empty the contents outside, fate took hold. The wind was in the wrong direction and my poor mum received what seemed like the entire contents, back in her face! I wondered if this was what was meant by 'what goes around comes around' but it did not seem to be the right time to ask!

It was when I was living in Hull when my real health problems started. I was admitted to hospital for an eye operation, which proved complicated, due to the intermittent air raids going on at the time. I survived but returned home much later than expected because of my illness. My mother again started to pick up the threads of everyday life, always waiting for more news of my dad. Another drama arose when my brother Bob contracted meningitis, which was a really serious illness to have in those days – it still is. It was touch and go and even mum feared for Bob, but he proved all the doctors wrong, slowly regaining his strength and returning to full health. The only thing he was pleased about was that there was no school for him and he took full advantage of the situation.

The war dragged on, and on many occasions we slept in the cellar, a normal occurrence for us, which we got used to. One night it was so cold that mum gave in and agreed to let us sleep in the warm living room, under the table. We were awoken by a loud explosion and had to make a dash for the cellar for the rest of that night, until the all-clear was sounded.

The cellar had many uses including our storeroom for coal. We had camp beds installed there, which we thought was great fun; it especially appealed to my brother and became a favourite place to spend time with his mates. One night after a hasty retreat into the cellar, my mother suddenly let out a terrible scream. She thought someone was hanging there! My brother had rigged up a broom, mop and my poor doll and suspended it from the ceiling to use for bayonet practice. My bother's bum was then the target for my mum's hand but the episode did not do much for my doll and she was never the same shape again.

It was the usual treat on a Saturday morning to go to the cinema, much to my brother's disgust, as this meant he had to take care of me. His choice words to me were, "Come on, you pest, don't ask to go to the toilet either, as I'm not taking you, so there." True to form, halfway through the matinee I needed the 'Girl's Room'. Bob stood at the top of the stairs refusing to come any further. All through my ablutions I kept calling, "Bob, are you there?" Then to his embarrassment I yelled at the top of my voice, "'Bob, I've wet my knickers!" He was not a happy brother and neither was I since I had to sit for another whole hour without any knickers on! With Roy Rogers on screen looking for a villain I decided I had had enough and said loudly, "Bob, have you still got my knickers?" It did the trick, for Bob dragged me out and away before his mates could see him. I learnt a lot from that episode.

Time passed and my brother and I grew up. Then came the great day when peace was declared, the war was over and dad was coming home! We lived in a street where all the houses were the same. A street party was arranged and all the children were seated at trestle tables, flags were flying, everyone was happy and the atmosphere was one of celebration and relief. Mum's factory job ceased. The American soldiers went home and were much missed, for they had certainly brought colour into a lot of lonely lives. It seemed ages after the street party, and still there was no sign of my father. Then one day, just as my mother was up to her arms in the washtub and Bob was off scrumping with his mates for apples, in walked this tall soldier. I was playing with our tabby cat in the kitchen and I remember seeing him come in and go straight to mum and give her a hug! "How dare this man hug my mum," I remembered thinking, and I hung onto her skirt as though to protect her. But yes, it was dad and how our lives changed from that day! He was a stranger to both my brother and me and it took us a while to get to know him. What upset Bob most was the discipline my father brought to the house. My brother could no longer play truant and get away with it, despite his best efforts. I thoroughly resented this man who now slept with mum as I was suddenly relocated to the back bedroom with my brother.

Gradually, a new way of life was formed. I started school. The highlight of my week was Monday morning when all the children took a penny for Sambo, a statue of a little boy who lifted his hand and when the penny was put into his hand, he then swallowed the coin. To this day I still do not know where the pennies went. I was five years old and it was normal for my mother to collect me from school. One day, aunty Alice came to collect me in her place. I panicked for I did not see her to start with. On the way to her house she told me that my dad was not well and that the doctor had been called. "Later," she said, "I will take you home." It was then I realised just how much I had grown to love him. He used to play games with me, draw special pictures and make me laugh. This was the dad I now remember. He never stopped showing us how much he cared and how much he loved us.

Aunty took me home and Bob was sent to get the medicine, which had been prescribed. I was really scared, for when mum let me look into the bedroom to see him, I remember he was sweating and shivering at the same time. They called the illness malaria, and it took my father some considerable time to get his strength back. No sooner had he recovered then he would get another bout of this horrible illness. Apparently, all the soldiers who were in the jungle in Burma were experiencing the same problem. It was a very frightening time for all the families because we were helpless; there was no medicine at the time that was effective when malaria struck, it just had to run its course. From that time on, I idolised dad.

My father managed to get a job as a chauffeur and we all moved to a neighbouring town. We lived in a tied house, which of course meant the house went with the job. It was not ideal, but dad was never out of work, so we had a rhythm and continuity in the way we lived. My brother became an apprentice plumber, which suited him; and he was good at it. However, he decided to join the Coldstream Guards and went to Australia for three years. We missed him, and it was during this period that I became very ill with rheumatic fever. It left me with a weak heart and St Vitus's dance, thus my next episode of learning. Just before my illness I had met my future husband, John, and we were planning our future together. By the time Bob returned from Australia, we were married! John and I were married in a traditional village church in Hartlebury, by the Bishop, who lived in the village. We were very lucky to find a cottage to rent and when I became pregnant, we felt our lives were truly blessed.

As my time got nearer, the doctor recognised that the baby was breech and would not turn. I was prepared for a bad labour, but not for losing our son. He was a full term baby and we were devastated by his loss. How could this happen to us? Why? I fought hard to understand and to let go of the bitterness, but we were both totally numb and the whole thing felt like a nightmare. Added to all this, at a time when I was still really weak and in shock, I followed a local custom to please my mother-in-law, who I held in high regard.

It was a tradition in those days that when a woman had given birth, she attended church for a blessing before entering other people's houses. The appointment was duly made and I attended. I was met by the minister and to my horror, he asked, "Where is the baby?" When I explained what had happened, I was even more appalled to be told that in no way could he give me this blessing because my child had been stillborn! I was completely devastated as if I had been struck through my heart, as if it was somehow my fault that God had given me this little son, only to snatch him back again. I looked at the minister and I wondered where the compassion was of this man who stood before me, who showed no sympathy, no warmth, no understanding – and this man was meant to be a man of God!

As I was standing there, words failing me, another lady came in with her baby for the blessing. She was not married, and yet she was given the privilege I was denied. It really was a hard lesson to start me on my journey of learning. I had been told too that there were not to be any more children because of the complications that caused my son's stillbirth. But soon I was expecting our second child. I remember going to the doctor who promptly said, "How did it happen?" I thought doctors knew these things! But he was very pleased for us and always gave me support, sensing that I was frightened of losing another child. However, this time it was fine, even though our new son picked up on my anxiety and was a cry-baby, night and day! We were blessed with another son, who was totally different, good as gold, and somehow the grief of losing my first-born faded and my faith was restored. The joy of joys came and our third son was born – three sons alive and a wonderful gift.

GOING ON

Years later something happened to me, which changed my life completely. I had been ill for a long time and everything seemed to be such a strain. Life was difficult for I was tired and lacked energy and I was experiencing a pain in my arms, chest and back. I believed it to be a reoccurrence of the rheumatic fever pains of long ago. However, after visiting a number of different specialists, I learned that the valves in my heart were failing. I was told that the only chance I had of prolonging my life would be open-heart surgery. I was thirty-two years old and did not want to die. The waiting list was long and it felt to me as if I would not even make it to surgery. The worry was overwhelming for us both as we thought of our three young sons. Who would look after them, what would happen to them? They needed me and I needed them and loved them so desperately. Again the question rose in my mind, "Why me?" I was only thirty-two but felt I had the body of a sixty-year old.

Two days later a letter came to tell me that a bed was available and that I was to telephone the hospital. After much heart searching and a lot of fear, I rang the hospital as instructed at 7.30am, only to be told that there was a shortage of blood and my admittance had been cancelled. This was not the best news and left me feeling somewhat on edge and very uptight. A week later I heard again, although this time by telegram. Same procedure, and I telephoned the hospital as instructed. I was told there was a shortage of intensive care nurses and my admittance was again cancelled. This was a real mental blow to me. I was beginning to wonder if it would all be too late; would I survive the delay?

At last another telegram came and the operation was definite. I remember saying goodbye to my children, choosing my words carefully – that they would be coming to see me in hospital. Upon admittance I was told that there would be a lot of tests before the operation, which made me rather fearful. Six months previously, I had experienced a painful procedure, the angiogram. I was pleased to learn however that these tests would be much easier and would take place the next day. The evening before the operation John brought my sons in to visit me and I saw my mum and dad. I asked them to look after the boys – if my operation was not a success. I knew what my chances were and it was a poignant moment when my family left.

When the surgeon came to see me, I remember thinking, "This man holds my life in his hands – and what big hands they are!" He explained the operation to me and I felt calmed by his relaxed attitude. He said, "My dear, put your trust in my hands and I will put my trust in God." I have never forgotten that man and I owe him my life. I remember saying to him, "Would my chances be any better if I had the one valve done?" to which he replied, "No, because under the added strain, the other one would collapse." There was no going back and all was set for the following morning. After the surgeon left I asked if I could go to the Chapel on my own. I felt I needed to talk in private with my Maker. I remember that I prayed as I had never prayed before. I prayed for my family to be able to cope, whatever the outcome of the operation and somehow I just knew that God had heard me. I felt better in myself, more at peace, and returned to the ward to try to get some sleep.

Morning came after a very long night yet somehow it came too soon. I awoke and remember thinking, "I wonder where I will wake up tonight?" Again my prayer was, "Please God, look after my family and give them strength whatever is to be." I felt that something had changed within me; I was aware of a different sense of 'knowing' and I was as ready as I would ever be.

I marvelled at how the nurses could be so bright and breezy. They were kind, just doing their job in the way they knew how, for it was an everyday occurrence for them, dealing with life and death. After the usual preparations were made, I was ready to go down to theatre. I felt so strange lying on my back. I hate to lie on my back! The anaesthetist met us at the door and was very reassuring, and then the surgeon came to squeeze my hand and give me the added confidence I needed at that time.

The surgeon's words were, "We will speak again soon, but the operation takes many hours." Little did he know then that twice during that time I was going to cause him great concern. I remember it clearly and understand now, what happened. During the operation, my 'inner me' stepped out of my body and hovered above the operating table. I travelled down a darkish, speckled tunnel, the speckles rather like shining stars. At the end of this tunnel was a wondrous light, so bright and so comforting. I remember that I was enjoying it. Suddenly, I stopped travelling, and in front of me I could see this familiar figure holding hands with a young boy. It was my grandmother, and with her was our son. I remember thinking that he looked about fourteen. The boy said to me, "Hello mum, I am Jonathan." In fact not a word was spoken for it was mind-to-mind communication. Gran just smiled and said, "Go back love, we are happy here." I was aware of other people in the background. They both smiled and my grandmother said, very clearly, "It is not your time. You must not come yet as it is not the right time." Back into my body I went – with a bump!

For a second time it was as if I had woken up and left my body behind on the bed. I was on my travels again and this time I travelled at great speed. Again, I was taken up this tunnel, which was so lovely and I remember it clearly. I reached the end of the tunnel too quickly and there in front of me were the most wonderful colours. I came face to face with this lovely being who said to me, "If you come any nearer our light, you cannot go back. Who will be there for your children? Go back child; it is not your time." Again I was back on the operating table.

People who do not understand ask me, "How could you know about that when you were completely under anaesthetic and being kept alive by machines? How can you remember seeing the operating table and the operating theatre?" I was aware of being in intensive care and of seeing my husband at my side. The nurse was telling him I was 'going' and that there was no more they could do. I distinctly heard this conversation. I thought I was talking to John, yet it was with thoughts, not words. The strangest thing of all was that I remember looking at the man I married some eighteen years earlier, not this older version! I knew that he was talking to me softly, lovingly, and privately.

Then I was away, back to this light, which was just so wonderful. This time there was no tunnel, just light. In front of me stood a figure, so bright and comforting, so incredibly loving, surrounded by a tangible love. I had absolutely no fear; I was just at peace with myself. I would never presume to say that this was God. The only thing I know is that this Being was love, joy, comfort and understanding. I was happy, relaxed and had no pain. I was told, "Go back, my beloved child, if you come any closer, you cannot go back. Work for Spirit and when the time is right, not one moment before and not one moment after, we will come for you. Go back; fulfil the plan of life that is your road to travel."

Two days later I was conscious, although still in intensive care. I was alive and I remembered it all so clearly. I always thought of 'Spirit' as being in a bottle! I had never really given much thought to the higher side of life. In fact I was far from being anything special, just a mother who had to bring up her sons, a very ordinary person. Surely I was not mad – I knew what I had seen and heard, but knew I would never be the same person again.

This is me, Margaret the person.

THE GIFT

The gift we offer to you is this
When the heart has no joy
We of Spirit
Give you hope
We give love, to sustain you
When there is not love
We offer consolation.

Every beat of the heart has its own message
Every tear tells a story
The heart cries, "please understand me"
The tear says, "love me"
The human asks, "Who understands me?"
This and much more Spirit does answer you.

Love cannot be measured
Life is not given to be easy
Your life has been given for a learning process
Learn well the human mind

Learn well the pitfalls of man
Earthly man can be blind.

Thirst for goodness
Hunger for compassion
Give compassion to others
Cry for mankind
Smile for the future
Give thanks for wisdom given to you.

Above all, rejoice in your knowledge, of a future, wondrous.
Above all
Look to a life to come, when man knows not sorrow
This is your Heaven
Your future assured.

I WAS NOW BEING MADE MORE AWARE OF MY FEELINGS AND INTUITION

Now I had time to take stock of myself; in fact I had died and found life. Soon I found the air in Kidderminster was not good for my breathing. Then Spirit started to take things in hand. My husband had to find another job; the house we had at that time was an ex-council house, which we were struggling to buy. It needed so much doing to it that we did not know which way to turn.

My parents were still living and I loved them dearly and John's parents had retired to Llandudno. He decided to try to find work in Llandudno, for three reasons:

The air would be good for me.

Our eldest son was about to finish catering college and, Llandudno being a seaside town, we thought the opportunities there would perhaps be better for him.

Houses in Llandudno were much cheaper than where we lived.

It seemed as though things were happening at a strange pace. I wondered what it was all about. My husband found a job after much searching and spent his nights looking for a house. He did not like being away from us and I must admit I was glad when he arrived home at weekends.

Fate took another turn and I awoke one morning with an urgent thought to go to Llandudno. This was a bit strange really and within ten minutes the phone rang. It was a friend of my mother-in-law, who said she was going to Llandudno for the day and would I like to go with her? Like a shot I asked my mother to watch over the boys and away I went. I did not have time to tell John, I thought he would welcome a surprise visit because I knew he was homesick.

We arrived in Llandudno and after visiting John's mother her friend said we would go and look around Conway; this is a beautiful place and the scenery and views are so special, not to mention the lovely castle. On the way back we took a wrong turn and ended in a cul-de-sac, where a lady was putting a notice in a house window – FOR SALE.

I could not believe my eyes, as the house seemed an answer to my dreams. Very cheekily I knocked on the door and the lady answered with the sticky tape still in her hand. She explained that only ten minutes before, she had received a phone call from the couple who were buying the house to say that their sale had fallen through, and they would have to back out. I asked (with my fingers crossed) what was the price. To my surprise, I knew we could scrape up enough. Now came the crunch; how long would she wait? The house had been left to her so there was no chain, which was a relief. As quick as a wink I telephoned my husband at his new job and arranged for him to join me. Within ten minutes we had settled the price and all that remained for me to do was to go home and put our house on the market. As we sped along the road, I wondered what this was all about. I had started out that day strangely and certainly finished it in an even stranger way.

Next morning I telephoned the local estate agent. He arrived at two o'clock in the afternoon. By four the house was on the market, sales board up and I prayed for an early response. It could not have been quicker. At five o'clock there was a knock on the door and a gentleman stood there and asked me about the house. I explained all and he promptly made an offer for cash. He wanted to move in as soon as possible, saying he had long fancied the house and had just come into some money.

Spirit was starting to pull rank and from then on, life changed. Soon we were moving to Llandudno, rather broke; we had to leave some of the furniture behind because it would cost too much to transport it. Never mind; my parents, years previously, had managed without chairs, so could we. The night before we moved, we stayed at my parents' flat and of course had to keep the cat in. The boys slept on the floor in sleeping bags and much to their disgust, at two in the morning, Kit the cat, decided that one of the sleeping bags was a toilet. Needless to say, we were wide-awake and ready to go long before dawn broke!

John was at work in Llandudno and we followed the removals van in my father's little car. The boys and I and a rather upset cat in the back seat; she howled and howled, so in the end we opened her basket and she sat, quiet as a mouse, on my lap for the rest of the journey.

I can never ever thank my special mum and dad enough for what they have done for me throughout all my life and I am a very lucky person to have had them for parents.

WE WERE IN LLANDUDNO

Sadly, no sooner had we moved to Llandudno than my father seemed to be going downhill; he was always tired and suffered internal problems. One day I received a phone call from my mum, telling me he was in hospital for observation, for what they thought was gallstones. Immediately I booked a coach seat and away I went, back to Kidderminster to see him.

I certainly was not prepared for what I saw. My father had aged in a matter of weeks. They were unsure whether the trouble was gallstones or not. I spent a little time with him but soon had to travel the 120 miles back to Llandudno, as I did not wish to leave the boys. Ken, our second son, was going for his first job interview, and like any mother hen, I wanted to be around. The next day I heard from the hospital that they were sending dad home. They said there was nothing wrong.

The following day my dad was admitted to hospital again. He was in agony, and an emergency operation was arranged for the evening. I threw some bits together and I was away again on the coach. I arrived in time to sit with him before he went down to theatre. My husband was on his way, but we knew it was not good.

After the exploratory operation we were called into the surgeon's room. He told us it was a question of hours, and that my dear dad was dying. He was riddled with cancer. I remember thinking, "Why, why should he be taken from me?" He was such a good man and it did not seem fair; he was only sixty-six. Because of his suffering I remember asking God, "Please don't let him suffer anymore. Take him home."

Dad regained consciousness at odd times. We all held his hand, hoping to give him some comfort, yet he was in a heavily drugged sleep. We stayed in relays around him. The nurse in charge of his care told us to go home and get some rest; he would be fine for a time. The family, my mother, brother, husband, sister-in-law and myself were just about to have a cup of tea when I heard a voice say with urgency, "Go back now." Without a second thought, I called to the family, "We have to go." We arrived just as his Spirit left his body. My dad was finally at peace and in no more pain.

I can't remember much about the funeral. My mother was devastated; she had no wish to continue. I remember her saying in her distress, "They might as well put me there." My brother and I had lost not only our dad, we had lost our best friend, who was always there for us. I know he is still around for me, he has proved it so many times, and just hours after his funeral, he came back to prove his love.

After we returned home from the funeral, I missed my dad so much that after two or three days I went to bed rather upset; I must admit I was in tears. Half way through the night, I awoke. The room was aglow.

There at the bottom of my bed stood my father. He sighed and said to me, "Titch (that was his nickname for me), "you are a silly girl. You should know I am all right. You have forgotten your tablets." Yes, I had forgotten those tablets that keep me alive. My reply was, "Oh thank you dad. Oh dad, you've come back." He smiled and the next minute he was gone. My husband stirred and said, "Who the Dickens has been smoking in here?" I replied, "Only my dad!" (both my parents were chain smokers).

FINDING OUT MORE

About this time, I got a job as a manageress in a local café-restaurant. In this shop we sold all manner of confectionery. I did not like the job and I liked the area manager even less, but because of money problems I had to work. So I continued until one day there was an almighty row and I blew my top.

I must admit, my feelings towards the manager and the Company at that time were not good. The area manager thought me a middle-aged frump. I suppose to his way of thinking I was. I went home and pondered the situation, and decided it was time to move on. The next morning I caught the bus earlier than usual and as I got off I felt the urge to look across the road. To my disbelief there stood the area manager. My first reaction was that the so-and-so had come to check on me and all the other staff. Then, strangely, I heard him call to me, "Very sorry, Margaret." That for a start seemed odd since he never called me by my first name, nor did he ever apologise to anyone. Then again, how did I hear him so clearly across a busy road?

I carried on to work, opened the shop and made sure the weekly figures were all ready to give to him when he came in. Time went on, until It was well past his usual time, in fact he was two hours late. The figures had to reach Head Office by 12 o'clock and still the area manager had not been in. I was about to call Head Office with the figures when the phone rang. It was the Big Boss. He said he had some startling news. "The area manager had died the previous evening at twelve. I said without thinking, "Are you sure?" "Without a doubt," he replied, "I have just come from his house." I now believe that when I saw him at 8.30 that morning, it was his Spirit maybe saying sorry.

To this day I have never heard anything more about him. I was sad for his wife and child, for he was only in his early thirties.

During this phase of my life I was so impatient. I needed to know to whom, what and where my life was taking me. I met some special people and attended the Methodist Church for the first time. I could not get away from the fact I was seeing Spirit so clearly, and having, so often, a foresight into things that were not of this realm.

One day I found myself sitting on the bus behind two ladies. They were talking about a medium who had great insight into the Spirit realms. My ears pricked up and I listened. I made a mental note of what they aid, including the medium's name and whereabouts.

As soon as I got off the bus I went to the phone box and looked this lady's number up and rang her. As soon as I spoke to her, I felt as though I knew her, although we had never met. She said that she would see me that Saturday. Little did I realise that this was the new beginning. I asked her how much the reading cost. It was not expensive, although at £5.00 it was beyond my means. I started to panic. Where would the money come from? We were broke and could hardly make two ends meet. Strange as it seems, I walked up the garden and there under the apple tree, was exactly the sum of money I needed, £5.00. It was in £1 notes, neatly rolled together. It certainly had not been there earlier, neither could someone have dropped it since we just did not have that sort of money. I started to feel guilty. Should I spend it on extras for the kids, or buy pumps for Andy, our youngest, who needed them? I stopped and thought. I had been given this gift for the reading, not a penny more or a penny less than was needed.

On Saturday I arrived at the medium's house and was shown up to her room. She was a motherly lady and I felt completely at ease with her. As soon as she spoke she said, "Hello dear, you are Margaret. I have been waiting for you." I thought, "I'm not late." How did she know my name? I had forgotten to give it to her on the telephone.

Then she proceeded to tell me about myself. I was bewildered. She spoke of my gran, who was also a medium, and of my journey into the Spirit realms. I was amazed. I told her how I felt about seeing the Spirit world and hearing them calling me. She smiled and said that she had been waiting for me for ten years and she knew all about me. I was going to carry on her work. I sat with my mouth open. Then, to crown it all, she told me how I had found the money for the sitting. It felt as though she had walked into my body. She said that now she could return home and although I did not understand at the time it was soon to become evident. She said I would have a hard time, yet I would work for Spirit. Her parting words were, "Remember that in the future, people will come to you with no money, only seeking help. Remember the gift of Spirit. For one day you will help others who have nothing." She would not take the money and told me to use it on the children. Needless to say, I did. I heard that two weeks later the old lady died in her sleep. God bless her.

From that time I started to know and work for Spirit the way they had sent me back to do so after my open-heart surgery.

ANOTHER EXPERIENCE IN MY LIFE

At this time, I was hungry for knowledge and could not find the help that I thought was there. I was vulnerable, easily hurt and afraid of being used and ridiculed. I joined many groups in order to develop my spirituality but found that the content was not always as spiritual as I had hoped. I found self-ego so strong, and jealousy harder to understand. Briefly I could not find my answer in the circles and development groups in those early years of seeking help.

At this time I had my first cancer problem. My arm was affected but luckily, with treatment, it was caught in time. I learnt another lesson. I was here on a learning path.

About the same time our first grandchild was to be born – joy of joys, our first granddaughter. We were so thrilled, at last a girl, and my mother was overjoyed. We had arranged for her to come over and see the baby. She was not well and we could not pinpoint what the problem was. My parents had been inseparable and we thought this would help her a lot, as she was so looking forward to holding her new grandchild.

Elaine and the baby were due home from the nursing home and mum was coming from the Midlands to spend a few days with us, and of course, to spoil the baby. Two days before her visit, she had a chance of a holiday. It was an old people's holiday and she was taking the place of someone who had cancelled. We urged her to go, for I thought she could come down the following week and still have the best of both worlds!!

Mum left to go on holiday on Saturday evening to a Pontin's hotel. She was due to arrive there about 5 o'clock. At six, after much spoiling of our granddaughter, it was time for her feed. I proudly gave her the bottle. At five past six an overwhelming feeling of love came over me. I started to cry, and felt a real fool, yet at that time I felt loving arms around me. I felt my mother so close that it felt overwhelmingly as if she was at my side with the baby.

Next morning I went to work, still very elated about being a grandmother. I worked in an hotel as an assistant manageress for the disabled. Suddenly the phone rang. It was my brother. I thought to myself, whatever had got him up on a Sunday morning? He asked me was I on my own at the hotel and I answered yes, apart from the chef who was preparing the food for the guests. He told me to sit down and be prepared for some bad news. I thought he was going to tell me that mum did not like her holiday and that she wished to come back. He then told me that mum had passed away at six the previous evening and he had not been able to contact me before as the hospital had only notified him at midnight. The feeling that I had had of my mother being so close to me, had happened in fact at the time she passed to Spirit.

She has since confirmed this many times.

The family bond that exists between mother and daughter is a wonderful thing. Until you have felt it you cannot understand the closeness of bonding. When my mother passed to Spirit I lost my best friend, and the sorrow I felt was because she had not seen her first great-granddaughter on the earth plane. As time progressed and my knowledge has increased, I understand she sees all and is always around the family if she chooses.

My first great-granddaughter was placed in my arms last year and as I touched her little fingers in wonder, I smelt my mother and sensed her behind me and I could smell the familiar smell of cigarettes. I heard her laugh and say, "Well Bab, we have done it at last." Indeed we had, great- great-grandmother, great-grandmother, and great-grandchild – SPIRIT AND FAMILY.

THIS POEM I WOULD LIKE TO DEDICATE TO MY VERY SPECIAL MUM

I was too late to say goodbye
I was not there, too late to say I love you Mum.
If I were there I could have held your hand as you passed to the
    other side
Forgive me Mum, I did not know your time had come
One minute alive next dead, alone in a hospital bed.
You have always been at my side when I needed you
It would have meant the world to me to be with you
When you needed me.
You loved me Mum as I love you
You, I know will be waiting for me
When I come home to you.

MUM'S HELP

It was a Thursday morning the same as always. As usual I seemed to be in a world of my own. "You will never change," my mother used to say. "You couldn't organise a booze-up in a brewery!" As I started to walk into the town, I had many things on my mind, trying to remember what I had forgotten. Sometimes I seem to walk in a dream and surprise myself when I get where I am supposed to be. This particular Thursday was no exception. As I stepped off the pavement I heard my mother in Spirit clearly shout, "Margaret, will you bloody learn!" I felt hands on my shoulders pull me back and stopped dead in my tracks. I was a second away from being knocked down by a coach. The driver was as shocked as I was. He shouted at me, "Mrs, if you wish to kill yourself, please don't do it under my bloody wheels!" I felt stupid.

I gave silent thanks to my mum. You see, my mother only ever really called me by my name when she was cross or worried.

Usually I was called by family nicknames, Bab or Titch, by my family.

Shaken, I arrived home to be met with a funny look from my husband who promptly asked where on earth I had been, as I reeked of cigarette smoke.

When I changed my blouse at night, I found two sets of three finger marks on my shoulders, again proving that love of Spirit never leaves you.

WARNING

I was going through a rough patch with heart problems and so was taking things very easy. This particular day started like any other day. I was standing at the sink washing up a few cups and saucers, when I looked around, and there stood my mother in very familiar clothes. I could smell tobacco smoke. She said to me, "Make yourself a cuppa, put your tablets in your handbag and everything will be okay." I never queried what she said at all, but I did what she told me to do.

As I sat drinking my tea there was a knock at the front door. I unlocked it, and my husband's boss was standing there, looking very strained and apprehensive. He then asked me to go with him to the hospital as my husband had had an accident and was still unconscious. He kept asking if I was okay. He could not understand that I had taken this news so calmly. We arrived at the local hospital where my husband was still having tests and was not yet conscious. I had to give them certain details and then wait.

The doctor came and said that my husband would be staying in hospital and that I could now see him. He advised me then to go home and ring later. On the way my husband's boss kept asking if I was sure no one had phoned me. To this I replied that I was sure. We, in those days, did not have a telephone. How can you explain to a man who thinks spiritualism is a dirty word? You can't. I think he still wonders to this day how I knew.

My mother in Spirit is still with me. She is at my side to give her love to me in many ways. Love does not stop when someone goes to the other realms.

MY THOUGHTS

I decided to seek help from the College of Mediumship, which was in Stansted, the finest place in the world to get the help and guidance I needed. A lady, who was a wonderful person of immense spiritual knowledge, talked to me through the meditation. I was overjoyed, and at last I came across in my mind again the Being I had met during my passing over. He spoke with truly wonderful compassion to me.

He said, "My beloved daughter, the road is set, do not be afraid. I will always be at your side. I will never leave you. When you call for me I hear. I will be with you to the end."

The emotions were so high with me I felt the tears running down my face. The lady who had taken the group spoke to me and she confirmed what I had heard and seen.

Yes, I had seen the most powerful wings that anyone could see. Yes, I still see those wings and when I need that extra help I visualise the protection of those wings.

After going home I seemed to be more in charge of myself, yet I still did not have the chance to work. At that time my husband's dad passed to Spirit, but no one believed what I did, it was never mentioned. After all the funeral arrangements we knew that I would be tied more to help John's mum. This I understood and she was in a great deal of pain with rheumatoid arthritis, progressively getting worse. She was a fantastic lady who never moaned, never ever wished to be a strain on anyone, in fact she was a rare, patient lady whom I did admire and love. Soon it reached the stage where she needed nursing home treatment.

One particular day we had been with mum for a long time and it seemed as though she was ready to snooze, so we made our way home. We had just arrived home and I let the cat out and put the kettle on. While I was doing this, I heard very clearly in my mind, "You must go back." I immediately called to John, my husband, not to lock the car, as we had to go back to the nursing home. He never queried my words and we returned to the home to find an ambulance parked outside. Yes, it was for mum, she had had a nasty fall out of bed and was unconscious. The matron was full of apologies about what had happened. We were then asked why we had not answered the phone when they rang us. Of course, the answer was we were already on our way back, thanks to my Spirit help – I had heard the message before it had been sent.

I travelled with mum in the ambulance and John drove behind. I was glad I was there because mum came round and was very frightened. She was a gentle, loving soul.

Time passed.

John's mother passed to Spirit but before she passed she asked John and me to look after her good friend May. I was already doing this at that time so I did not see any new major problems. I thought that perhaps time would now be on my side.

Again, I was wrong. As time went by May's health deteriorated rapidly and as much as I loved May, she could indeed be rather awkward. This I put down to a very unhappy life. May had no one. Her much loved and only son had died when he was eleven from a brain tumour, caused by a ball hitting him on the head. He would have been my age now. May's husband Joe was also in Spirit so she was alone and not a happy person. Very much used to having her own way, that was May, yet I really thought of her as a second mum.

John and I decided to go on holiday. May's only child, her son David, was buried in Southampton so we decided to go to the surrounding area to try to find his grave. He had been buried there about fifty years ago, which is a long time for a grave to be unattended.

A day of our holiday was destined for that purpose and we duly set off. It was a lovely day as we boarded the train. Upon arriving at the station we stopped and bought some flowers in the hope of finding the plot. I had already told May our plans and she was overjoyed to think we could locate his grave. All May had was a plot number, and she said the grave was on a slope and had a black vase with the inscription, 'David our son'.

We arrived at the cemetery and went to the office there. To our dismay it was locked. The notice read that they were only open on Thursdays. We were so despondent; no way could we find the grave without help. All May knew was a date, so we decided we would have to try another day.

Then we heard a coughing inside the office door and chanced our luck. Indeed we were very lucky. The cemetery superintendent was calling at the office to pick up some papers. He kindly opened the door and we explained our problem. As he said, fifty years for an unattended grave was a long time, a lot can happen in that time, especially as there was no marker stone. We explained what we knew and all that May had told us. We also mentioned the black vase that had David's name. He then so kindly telephoned into town and we waited patiently for some directions of where to start our search. The clouds had suddenly turned black and we realised how silly we were not to have come prepared for the weather change; we had not thought to bring wet weather gear. The superintendent smiled at us and directed us to an old part of the cemetery.

We started our long search. First we had to find the area, then the row, and finally the plot. Three hours later we were no nearer to finding the grave, when something strange happened. I heard a voice say, "Look over there where there is a new patch." So I did as I was told. Sure enough I found a re-opened grave with some flowers on it. I could not believe what I was being shown. Next to it was the numbered area we were looking for.

It was completely overgrown and there was no sign of the vase. Again I heard a voice say, "Look," and down the slope on its side was the vase. I ran down to it and carried it back and, after much rubbing with wet wipes, the name was clearly visible. Yes, it was the correct stone vase and it had obviously rolled away when the grave next door had been opened.

We did the best we could and replaced the vase and flowers with pride. I knew that May would be overjoyed and we were so happy to have done this for her. We took photos, which she treasured for the rest of her life, she was so happy. She took these photos with her into the Spirit world.

As we left the grounds the heavens opened and it poured with rain. We then continued with our holiday. That night I telephoned May to tell her the good news. She was so happy she cried. We found the grave thanks to the goodness and help of the Spirit world.

One day while visiting May in the nursing home, I had this strange feeling that I had to get home quickly. Instead of waiting for a lift as I usually did, I rang for a taxi. This was cutting my visit short, yet I knew I had to get home quick. I arrived home and thought to myself, what an idiot I was, what was the matter with me? I thought, well, I am here so I might just as well do some typing. I duly started and had been working for about an hour when there was a terrific bang. A new neighbour came and was knocking frantically on our door. She said that the windows in the house of my friend, Ann, who lived in a bungalow across the road from us, had just been blown out. I ran over and could see smoke coming from the kitchen. I knew that my friend was inside. I shouted, but I could not see her. By this time my husband had run over to the bungalow and I told him to ring the emergency services, as there was a smell of gas. I finally located my friend, who was smouldering and was not a good sight. Within three minutes all services arrived. I found the hardest job was to stop Ann tearing her clothes off. She had a nylon dressing gown on and had been working nights, and got up to make a cuppa. The gas boiler had been leaking and I understand the spark from the kettle had done its worst, thus the explosions.

Ann was in a critical state and she was fighting for her life. I found it strange to think that I had coped with this terrible thing as I had only just got over a bad heart turn. Yet I do believe that Spirit in its own way had sent me home early that day.

All the following year was trial and hardship for my friend. Her hands were like lumps of leather and she had lost all confidence in herself. In a way she was a lucky girl, she had a husband who adored her and she gave so much love to other people and unlimited love to her animals.

As time progressed my friend got worse. There seemed no relief and the hospital system did not seem to be helping. It was hard for her friends to see her suffer yet it was agony for her husband. I did my best to keep an eye on her and offer support.

MAY'S PASSING

I was going through a bad time when I did not feel well and felt very frustrated. I did not seem to be any nearer my goal of working for Spirit. It was one step nearer, then two back. I never seemed to have enough hours in a day, nor enough time to spend with my family. In fact, very frustrated with my lot, I wondered if I would ever really work for Spirit.

It was a Thursday afternoon and I usually went to see May that day. I did not feel well and so I telephoned her and said that I would be there the next morning instead about 10 o'clock. I told her that I had the biscuits I always brought her, and some other bits and pieces she loved.

Next morning I got ready and was just about to start out when the telephone rang. It was the nursing home asking me to go to the undertakers to identify May's body, as she had died around midnight. I could not believe what I was hearing. Why had they not sent for me? I was classed as her next of kin and was responsible for her, yet they had deliberately not told me. I was so angry; I should have been notified, not to mention that in another five minutes I would have been on my way to the nursing home.

I was also so upset that after being with her three times a week and always being at hand I had not perceived this coming. Of all the premonitions I had, I was not aware of this one.

After much confusion the day and time was set for May's funeral. The money side of the situation was a problem but eventually it was all sorted out. On the day of the funeral we arrived back from the crematorium to our house to find police cars, ambulances, a fire engine and a lot of activity opposite in my friend's bungalow. Terrible fear came upon me.

My friend had suffered pain beyond belief after the gas explosion; she could not stand the pain anymore and felt she was a burden.

I had lost two good friends in one week. I felt so guilty that I had not been there for Ann, as I was dealing with May's funeral, and had not seen my friend for four days. The pain she suffered was unbearable and she could take it no longer. She took her own life. At that time I blamed myself for not seeing the situation, yet I understand that the gifts Spirit has given to me are not for my use, only for spirituality.

I was then offered the first chance to work on platform.

It was the day of Ann's funeral, and this was the day I was booked to do my first demo. Let me explain. It takes years to be asked to work. Sometimes these are very closed shops, but everyone needs the first chance to work and sadly not all mediums will open doors for others. I was lucky, I had met a lady named Agnes at my Stansted visit, who offered me this chance and I knew that once that happened, I would be on my way. Still to this day I work with my friend Agnes and we have had many experiences and happenings working with the world of Spirit. I admire her work and will always be grateful for her giving me my first opening.

As it happens I was at a well-known church in Liverpool. To

someone like me, a newcomer, it was a challenge and a very frightening thought to be thrown in at the deep end – I think that is the expression.

To make it worse, it was the day of my friend's funeral, of all days. I was torn, should I go or not? Yet I knew if I did not I might never again be given the chance. After much soul searching I found my answer, yes, I would go and work, this is what my friend would have wished. She knew all about my interest. So my husband and family went to the funeral and I went to demonstrate. I must admit I was a bag of nerves, not confident at all. My fears were what would happen if I ran dry or worse still, not receive anything? All this and more was going through my mind. I tried to think positively, tried to remember to trust in Spirit. I had my misgivings and wondered at my own sanity.

The demo started and I felt my legs turn to jelly and my heart thumping. I faced the sea of faces, and I wanted to run. As sure as anything, if I had had a bottle of whisky with me I would have drunk it. Sadly, or luckily, I did not. Then I put out a prayer and as I did so I asked for help – gosh, I needed it.

Then to my amazement I looked to the centre aisle. There stood my friend Ann, looking radiant. She put up her hands and called to me, "Hi Marg, I'm fine, it's wonderful here, mate, look at my arms, look at my hands!" I did and they were perfect, no scars, no horrible burn damage. She looked a million dollars. She laughed and called to me, "Go on Marg, wow them. I am here for you. See you again soon."

At that precise time the mourners would have been leaving the churchyard. I thanked her with all my heart. I thanked all my Spirit helpers and then the evidence flowed. I was ready at last for working with Spirit. I was so happy that my friend understood and since that day, she often comes around, always when I least expect it.

THE TRAIN RIDE

Once again, I was on one of my travels to the Midlands.

I started out to the station and I was thinking of all the mental work that I would do. Strange as it may seem to anyone else, I find I very often receive some very special inspirational work on a train. Not this time. I was settled, wriggling around like a mother hen, ready for a comfy ride.

I had been on the train about an hour when two dear old people got on and settled opposite me. I remember thinking how happy they looked. Then the noise started, as the door to the coach part kept banging. It was really getting to me, so I decided to move further down the train. That's where I was wrong. As I stood up to move I felt a distinct push to sit back in my seat. Then I heard, "Fred is fine, but his wife is not." My reaction was, this is ridiculous, but looking across it was very noticeable that the old lady was in trouble. I was told there was an angina spray in the old man's pocket. Asking the old man if I could help, it was obvious he was very frightened. When I mentioned the spray to him he couldn't think, then he remembered it was in his pocket for safety. By this time I could see this was no ordinary angina attack. I said to him, "Don't worry Fred, I'm going to get some help." His wife was hardly conscious.

After I found the guard and explained, he followed me up the coach of the train, whereupon he telephoned ahead for an ambulance to meet us at the next station. So my new friends were being helped. As the old man neared the door, he turned and asked me how I knew his name was Fred.

Soon they were being whisked away to hospital. As the guard came back on the train he said the old man had asked him to say thank you to me, and had said that God had sent me to sit by them that day. Once again, I said a big thank you to Spirit for its wisdom.

After the first demo was over, I wondered if it would be the last, which says I soon learnt to trust Spirit. The next working demos were booked and I found myself being asked to work in churches. I thank my friend Ann from the Spirit realms. My road was set. About a month after she went to the Spirit World, I awoke one morning not really feeling myself, so I made a cup of tea and was basically looking at nothing from the lounge window. Then sure enough, I saw her, holding her cat in her arms. She smiled at me, and I thought to myself, what on earth are you doing up at this time? Then of course it dawned on me, she was in Spirit. About an hour later her husband called at the door, "Margaret, don't look for the cat to feed her, she died this morning," and to this I honestly replied, "Indeed yes, Ann came for Tibs the cat." She now has her cat with her.

I have seen my friend since. Once when I was gardening I looked up and she was standing by her gate. She smiled and waved and disappeared. Perhaps I will one day see her form again, time will tell.

TREATMENT

I was feeling very sorry for myself, very defeated, as one more blow I had to cope with was having a ten-day course of radiotherapy. If you have not been in this position it is not easy to explain the feelings that accompany this treatment. I hate being closed in at any time, and It did not make it very easy once the door of the treatment room shut. It was my last day of treatment and after the first few days every session seemed harder to cope with. I remember lying on the couch not being able to move. It was most important to keep still. I am a very awkward person who finds it very hard to stay put for more than five seconds. Perhaps it was my nerves that made me start to panic. I had recited my maths tables, said the Lord's Prayer and recited nursery rhymes, but still there was time left. I remember calling out loud in desperation, "Mum, if ever I needed you, this is one of those times." From nowhere I felt my mother's hand upon my shoulders, I could smell the familiar smell of cigarettes and I knew she had heard my call for help. I remember hearing her say, "Don't worry anymore Bab, I am here. I will stay with you, and it will soon be over." I murmured, "Thanks mum."

When the radiographer came in to the room she laughingly said to me, "I don't understand, you told me that you did not smoke." "That is so," I answered. "Well," she said, "can you explain the smell of cigarettes everywhere?" She was a very sensible lady, and I pondered whether to try and explain to her. Then I thought better of it. My mum is around me, that I know and when I need her support, she always hears my plea for help.

JOY

On one of my visits to my family's graves, I had the overwhelming urge to find a little girl's resting place. This little one lived next door to us when we lived in the Midlands. She was a lovely child and years previously she had been killed tragically in an accident, when she was crushed. She was a very sweet child and in the early years of my illness she would come and sit and talk to me and I found her company a real joy. She was just four years old when she died.

Years went by and I never forgot her. She used to call me aunty Maggot because it was her way of saying Margaret. During a quiet time one night I distinctly heard her call me. She said, "Hello aunty Maggot, it's my birthday." Then I knew that when I next went to the cemetery I would look for her grave.

Now she and her family were strong Catholics and at the time of the funeral I was again going through a bad patch so I was not present. For that reason the next time I was in the Midlands where she was buried, I went to find her grave. I explained to the caretaker that I was looking for the Catholic part of the cemetery. He said it was on the high ground and he knew no more. I then started my search. With flowers in hand, again it seemed a long search, yet I knew I had to try. After about five minutes I heard a voice say to me, "Look over there to the left, the far end." This I did, and walked straight to the grave. I

40

looked at the headstone and all the memories of her laughter came back. I put the flowers on the grave and heard someone say, "Thank you, aunty Maggot." I knew it was this very special child talking to me.

Two weeks later I was attending a meeting when a medium came to me and said she could hear someone laughingly calling me Maggot. What more proof of survival could I ask for?

This poem is dedicated to a special child, a little angel loaned from God.

LITTLE ONE

Little ray of sunshine
A beam of light from heaven above
Nestled on a special child at play
The light shone on her brown curls
Her innocence radiates from deep within
She asks no favours, this special child of God
No earthly possessions did she have
She knew not greed neither strife
In her short earthly life.
She was loaned from above, giving to others love
The summer in her smile brightened even the darkest day
She came for a little while to share her light
Not long after that summer's day she returned to the
Perfect life to live and play.
We miss her, we loved her so we constantly asked God why
Why did she have to go?
The answer came from our desperate plea
We heard our answer clear
She is in no pain she has no tears or sorrow
With God above she lives
She shines from above to light the way for other children
Who come her way in future days.

THE BROKEN WINDOW

I was ready for a new session at the College of Mediumship, which I needed to recharge my batteries. I duly arrived. I was on my own yet I always soon made friends. I met a lady and we seemed to gel together; her name was Becky, and immediately we became good friends. We were nothing alike, yet we were both seeking knowledge. She had the brains that I so sadly did not have, she was a very clever lady.

During our time we enjoyed some lovely spiritual experiences. One that particularly stayed in my mind was when we sat in the chapel together, and I was feeling rather disturbed. I sensed glass splintering and grew uneasy. I said to my friend, "Let's not sit by the window tonight as the wind is blowing." Nothing different happened, and I began to think I was again going over the top in my imagination.

Next morning I telephoned home and asked my husband if there had been any problem with broken glass. He seemed startled and replied that our son had tripped and fallen into the glass coffee table. He was not hurt, yet the table was a wreck. The table did not bother me, as long as the lad was safe. Again Spirit and its thoughts had been relayed.

THE HOUSE

Not so long ago we decided to move home. Well, if you have done it you can understand the pitfalls during the lead up to the sale and how you sometimes wonder why you are bothering. After a troubled time of no sale we decided to sit back and lick our wounds. After six months, again we decided to put our home on the market.

This time it was one of those sales when the buyer wanted it very quickly so we agreed. Then big trouble started; we were gazumped over the property we wanted, and things did not turn out well.

Being me, and very fed up, I started to moan at my Spirit helpers and I asked for help. Their answer was, "Wait, trust. Look for the cross." I thought, "This is fine for them. I am human and have a house full of furniture, an old cat and nowhere to go." A week was left but we decided that we had to keep to our agreement and move. It was strange really because I sat in the afternoon near to tears and wondered why I was trying to serve Spirit when all that seemed important to me was going wrong.

Some friends asked me if I would like to meet up for a drink and a chat. Why not, I thought, a laugh is what I need. The girls asked me if I had found anywhere to live. My reaction was, "Have I hell!" One of the girls mentioned a bungalow of her late mother's that she had to sell, and whether I had seen it. I said, "No," and she offered to rent it to us. I could not understand how I had not seen it in the estate offices. We agreed that I would talk to my husband and meet them the next day.

Our idea was to rent until we were sure. We arrived and went into the bungalow. Probably the photograph had put us off. Once inside it seemed bigger than it was and we decided on a quick sale for cash. Within a week we were in. We went to the bottom of the garden, and in line with us was a boundary line of hedging to the nursing home. There at the centre stood a cross on the wall (so be it).

MY SPIRIT FRIENDS

Voices I hear are clear to me
The things I see are shapes of eternity,
A gentle touch to make me aware
My friends of Spirit are there,
Words of comfort they do share.

I smell the fragrance of a long ago memory,
A smile, a laugh, a word known only to me.
These are the thoughts
I receive from beyond this earthly realm
Certain proof of a future bright, in the hereafter life.

When the earthly body is needed no more
Then Spirit enters God's open door.
This is our eternity.
Together again, forward we go
To meet our loved ones of long ago.
This is the gift of life promised,
This is the certain knowledge of life eternally.

THE CAT

It is strange, because I really know that animals have a strong feeling of awareness, but one thing that sticks in my mind is whenever I have had off days, my cat seemed to understand and would stick very close. I noticed that when I was receiving treatment at the cancer unit, my cat knew what I was going through. She would go to the end of the drive and sit for about an hour before the transport arrived bringing me home. Then she would follow me in and wait outside the bedroom door while I slept. When I got up she would then follow me, and then and only then would she eat her food. This scenario lasted until my treatment had finished.

Animals are much wiser than us. One particular day I was very concerned about the old cat. She was not eating and seemed to be deteriorating, her eyes were so dull and I knew she had rheumatism by the way she walked around. I dug deep in the garage and got the old cat basket out. All the way to the vet she howled and created a terrible din. I felt like a traitor, yet I thought it was time for her to sleep.

We arrived at the vet and she would not come out of the basket. Finally we got her out, much to her disgust. The vet spoke reassuringly to her but it cut no ice. He amazed me by saying, "Take her home, she will go in her sleep. If you are worried, I will come out and help her." So we took her back home. The faggot was out of the basket in a flash and as much to say, "I fooled you," commenced to eat and eat.

Another of her tricks was when I was doing readings; very often she would come and sit outside the door. At odd times she would come into the room. One time sticks in my mind; she saw a Spirit cat with a lady who I was reading for and to my embarrassment, she turned and ran up the hall tiddling all the way. She kept well away from my room for a couple of days.

Cats are very knowing. Even the cat we had before knew exactly at what time the boys were leaving school. She would wait for them on the corner of the road. Nothing would move her, and even when the boys grew up she would know the sound a distance away of one of the boys' mopeds.

This is the wisdom of so-called 'dumb' creatures – to me they are anything but dumb.

Truthfully and maybe to play a better part in our future existence, like most people there came a time in my life when I had to make a decision about my special cat. Kit was old, her sight was going, and there was no pleasure in her life. She had difficulty moving and could not eat anything but the jelly of the cat food. I knew because I loved her I could not see her suffer like this. Strangely, it was on my birthday that I had to make the decision and I took her to the vet who confirmed my fears. And so she was helped to sleep. I brought her home, crying all the time. I know I should know better there is no death even for a loved animal, but I am human. We buried her in the garden, at her favourite spot, yet I could not bear to think of her little body out in the cold. At that time I forgot what I preach to others or perhaps I was so overcome with grief that I was wrapped up in my own sadness, but it was not a happy birthday!

The following week we went on holiday. Even then there were times I realised she would not be here when I returned.

The body is in a shell, which holds the earthly parts of life. When the body has ceased to function it is time for the soul to move on. We know the body is an overcoat, so why do we mourn? The body is the physical remains, and it is the soul which we should rejoice in. At the time of our passing we are reborn; there is no death, only life eternal.

The memories we have on earth are ingrained on other people's lives, yet what is life? Life is a span of time from conception to end and during that lifetime we learn who we are, what we are and why we are. It is not an easy lesson but it is a lesson we must learn. We must seek the knowledge to go further into a higher dimension. When we meet our God, our maker, then we are accountable for our lives. I strongly believe that God does not judge us harshly, yet we judge ourselves according to our lives. At our time of passing we then understand our purpose. Perhaps our life has been for the good of others. We have lived to learn a lesson ourselves. No one is perfect, and no one is better than any other person. But we are assured our God loves us and accepts our human faults. It is up to us on earth to attain the more spiritual progress, so that at the end of our days on earth we know ourselves, and we can judge ourselves honestly.

When we returned from holiday the house seemed empty. You cannot have a cat for 18 years and not love it. I went to bed that night after asking the Spirit world for help over a church matter, asking for guidance. The answers did not seem clear. I finally went to sleep, a restless sleep, and then my legs and my feet were aching. I felt a weight upon my feet and I looked down the bed and there was Kit curled up on my feet. She got up, stretched, walked up the bed and sat by my elbow. I stroked her for I felt the beat within her of her heart and I said to her, "You shouldn't be here," because my husband didn't like animals on the bed. Fair enough, and for that split second I forgot my special cat was dead.

Needless to say I cried, yet I know she understood and she was all right. Another week passed and I wondered if I would ever see her again. I went to bed and no sooner had my head touched the pillow than I heard her purring and felt her jump on the bed. I could not see her. Again as I cried, she remembered when I felt ill, and comforted me. I know I will see her again, another time, another place.

THE FUNERAL

During the course of the work I do, I can truly say every day is different. The first funeral I ever worked at was for a gentleman I believe was 96, yet he died a very lonely old man. He had a nephew and I understand this was his only family. It is very hard to talk about someone you have never met and I had never met this old man. He was a spiritualist. If I had known about him I would have made it my business to visit.

I asked for guidance from the Spirit realms. I was told to read a poem that I had been given a long time before called The Tree. This poem speaks of man's life that is likened to a tree.

THE TREE

A man's life is like a tree
From the roots
Grows the trunk giving
Life to the branches
The branches support the twigs that flower
This is the fruit of life
The roots are the foundations
Firm in mother earth

Then the trunk
This is as the spine
That supports growth
The twigs and flowers wither
When life's span finished
The branches age
The trunk ceases to hold life
Still the roots remain
These are the foundations of life
Memories left on earth long after the body has ceased to exist.

The service was organised, and all the arrangements were completed with the undertaker. On the day of the funeral I arrived at the crematorium as is policy in plenty of time. In due course the cortege arrived, with only the deceased, the nephew and two carers. How sad to think that this was the old man's only mourners. During the service I heard distinctly a harsh voice call, "Hey missus!" I was cross, how dare anyone shout like that. Yet in fact the person had every right – he was the deceased, it was his funeral. He was sitting on the edge of his coffin swinging his skinny legs. He said, "Tell them about my Lizzie. Tell them we had a son who had diphtheria when he was four. Now I am with them I am really, really happy."

Then with a giggle he said thanks to the girls and apologised for the bruises. These girls were his carers.

After the service the nephew said the usual thanks and said he was so glad I had the letter. He wondered if I would get it in time. "What letter?" I asked. He said, "The one with the details about my uncle's son." To this I honestly replied, "I have received no letter." His reply was, "Well, where did you get your information?" I said that as soon as I got the letter I would send it back to the undertaker unopened and this I did. The girls laughed about the bruises, "Yes", they said, "he used to pinch our bums when we passed his chair." I should say this, the man was happy. He was not lonely anymore, he was with his loved ones and had just come to tell us that. As soon as he gave his message he was back to where he belonged, with his family.

MEDIUMSHIP WORK

To any aspiring medium I strongly say, don't think it will be easy, because it will not. You are very lucky if you are given a chance to work since many newcomers to the world of platform very rarely do. Thus, it is not an easy road to travel, and few mediums are given the opportunity to prove that they do communicate with the Spirit world.

Life moved on, and I at times was ready to forget all about the business of mediumship, as It did not seem to bring me much personal joy. My mum was always with me, this I knew as increasing awareness of the Spirit realms unfolded. I knew deep in my heart that my parents were happy together at last. I asked Spirit frequently for guidance to follow the correct path and believe me, did I have some setbacks! I was soon to realise that people I thought were spiritual could easily deceive and use me, then use me again for other people's energies to drain me.

Only knowledge and the awareness of protection and self-preservation can pull you through the trauma of proving true dedication.

GHOST

During the time I was bringing up my children and working when I could, I found a job I thought would not be too strenuous. It was as a representative for a hosiery firm. All the new employees at some time were to go to Head Office, then on to the factory to learn how the products were made.

There were about eight of us from all the areas. We arrived as planned at the hotel, where rooms had been reserved for us by the Company. I seemed to get on well with one of the girls, and we went around together. She was a divorcee, and could not really understand how I missed my family. We were there for three days. On the second day we attended lectures and then in the afternoon we were all busy being shown the workings of the factory. I must admit I was tired, although I enjoyed the luxury of the hotel, as I had never been spoilt like that before.

During the evening we were left to our own devices. We sat in the bar contemplating where the local cinema was. One of the area managers came up to us and asked my new friend if we would like to go out for the evening. It was not me he was interested in, I knew, so I said to her that if she wished I would go to bed with a nice drink and catch up on some paperwork. She was very keen to go out. I said to her that I would stay awake and listen for her return, then we could have a talk. She said she would be in about midnight. Why not? She was a free agent.

By about one o'clock I was a little concerned for her. My room went very cold and I remember looking at the door, which I thought was open. I really should have known better because I had locked it. Across the room a young woman was walking, and I looked and looked again. I thought she was in fancy dress. When I spoke to her she looked at me, so sadly, and walked outside through the window. As she passed the dressing table the whole mirror had misted over. I felt physically sick and I was so cold. Then reaction set in, and I was furious. How dare anyone be so stupid and play practical jokes at this time of night! I turned the gas fire up and made a cup of tea, then waited for my new friend to get back.

Next morning after a sleepless night, I decided to go and complain to the hotel management. I walked down to the reception desk. The receptionist was just coming on duty and immediately she had a tongue-lashing from me. The fact that I was worried about my friend being out all night did not help. The young girl on the desk was visibly shaken. I said that I did not think it a good policy for guests' keys to be used for practical jokes. She assured me that only the hotel manager had access to the master keys after nine o'clock, and she would go and get him. I explained to the receptionist and the manager what had happened the previous night. I was then asked if I wished to change my room, as there had been a similar occurrence before. It was disclosed to me that the room I had was over the old stable, where a serving girl had been murdered by a groom long ago.

My new friend had had a wonderful time and had stayed the night with her new date. Me, I'd had a very restless night with a ghost and I was quite relieved to be going home that evening for a rest.

PROOF OF SURVIVAL

There are many ways that proof of survival can mean so much to a person. It is often the little things that can speak of survival, perhaps a pet name, maybe a positive thought of Spirit or even a saying, this is what we call medium's love. This is proof that cannot be denied, a familiar habit known only to the close family of Spirit.

There have been many ways that Spirit has really shown me how correct and eager it is to work with us.

One day I had a phone call from a gentleman asking if he could come and see me. I always ask if they understand that I am not a fortune-teller, but that my job is to prove survival. To this I received a very strong, "Oh yes, that is what I wanted." I never advertise what I do, I have never had the need, as all my readings are from word of mouth to me, which has always been sufficient.

I, as usual, went into the room to prepare before the reading. Before I work I like to play music, which to me is the best way of tuning in. Immediately I felt a very strong presence. A young man told me his name and held out a rosary to me. I thanked the young man, who was so eager to come and talk with me. Within a few moments a knock came on the door, and before me stood a very good-looking man, very smart. I felt at ease but I sensed he was a little on edge. My Spirit friends were with me, by this I mean my Spirit helpers. As I looked at the gentleman it seemed as though Spirit changed his clothes. He worked, in my clairvoyance eye, in priest's robes. We started to talk, and I told him that what we spoke of was given with love from the Spirit world. For a time we spoke of religious matters, and he asked a lot of questions. I answered to the best of my ability, telling him about my life as a spiritualist and my experience of passing over. I thought it was perhaps what he needed. Spirit had taken a hand and was leading to the purpose of his visit. I then told him of the people I felt drawing close to him. I spoke firstly of the young man who was waiting so patiently to speak to him, at which point my client broke down and cried, but not with sorrow, it was with joy.

Our Spirit friend gave him positive proof of who he was and why he went to the world of Spirit. Sadly for my client, when he did it seemed to matter what his religion was. "We are all children of one God," were the parting words from the young man in Spirit. "I am with God, not in hell, the hell I found was on earth. Our God is love, I am happy, I am with family, and all is well till we meet again. I give my special love to you my partner." To me, this was a very emotional reading. No matter what coat we wear or what banner we fly, we are as one in Spirit.

HOUSE CLEARANCE

You are wrong in thinking that this means moving places or furniture. In fact, it means moving troublesome Spirits who for their own reasons do not wish to progress. This work involves strength of character and the knowledge that Spirit is protecting you. By this I mean one's own helpers.

One needs a very strong protection. I believe in the power of prayer and of course the presence of guardian angels. I myself always call upon them for their wisdom and guidance. Strange happenings do happen and if there is any weakness on the part of the medium shown, this can work against the energies. As experience grows it is easier to adapt to the different energies around when working, but no two jobs are ever the same.

I was asked to visit a house in which the feeling, according to the agent, was not good. He was rather perturbed about going in on his own. This I could well understand, as in this particular place there had been a murder.

I asked my two good friends to accompany me and the estate agent and we all went to the house. Understandably no one would accept the job to clean the property. All the furniture was still there and the gloom around the house was deep. I felt a presence where the person had been bludgeoned, and there was still a trace of blood on the wall. Soon we pieced the story together. We asked this Spirit to go to the light and we felt the house was a happier place.

All seemed well, and it was, we thought, time for us to go. We moved towards the door, but it would not open. We tried forcing it, then we tried a knife, still it would not budge. The estate agent was looking a bit pale and I must admit my two medium friends and I were not happy.

I felt the urge to turn around and there in the kitchen was a remarkable light. It shone as much as to say, thanks, and the door opened wide. I must confess we did not linger, yet we all knew that there would be no more trouble. All was well, and the property was cleaned and sold in due course. No more strange feelings.

A FRIENDLY VISIT

Some time ago, at the end of last year, I was invited by a colleague to visit her father who had very limited time, was in much pain and who was riddled with cancer. This poor man lay for almost all of his time in bed, ready to die. He said he was ready to go but that he was waiting for someone. When it was time he knew he would go but he was getting weaker and weaker. Sometimes we do not know what to say or how to say it but I knew this man to be a man of God, a man who believed in life after death and a man who was nearing his transition.

Upon entering his room he smiled at me and said he knew I was coming. I thought this strange for my colleague had not told her father anything about me and she said he would probably think I was a social worker. I held this man's hand, so gnarled and thin, and my heart went out to him for I had seen my own father die of cancer and all the memories came flooding back. He nodded to me, this gentleman, and looked at his Bible at the side of his bed and asked me to read to him. I must explain this – without my reading glasses I cannot see to read a thing. I did not wish to disappoint him and much to my surprise, I opened the book as a matter of course, and started to recite the 23rd Psalm. I don't know how I remembered it but it came word for word. I cannot explain it to this day but I felt at peace. At the end he squeezed my hand, tears running down his face, and he said, "Thank you my dear, thank you, I am ready."

As I turned, over my left shoulder I could see a young boy about seven years old, at the back of me. At one side of him was an older man who said his name was Roy, and on the other side an older lady who said her name was Gwen. I said to my friend as he lay in the bed that these three people were giving him love. He smiled, sighed and closed his eyes and murmured, "I have been waiting for my boy," for the young lad was his son. I tiptoed out of the room hoping I had brought him some comfort, but I was very emotional, for as I looked at this gentleman, I relived my own torment of seeing my dad in the same state. I returned home that night, and when I came into my room to put some books away I felt compelled to look at the clock; it was a quarter to eight. I noticed the presence of someone behind me, and it was the gentleman I had previously visited. He was laughing and he was happy; there was no pain in his face and all he said was, "God bless you love, I'm fine!"

I then rang my colleague who was out. I left a message saying that I understood and at a quarter to eight, all was well. Next day she telephoned me to tell me that at precisely sixteen minutes to eight o'clock, her father had died.

READINGS

Sometimes when one gives a reading you receive a message that seems so silly, it is hard for reason and mind to differentiate.

A very unusual clearance is always given for a reason, even though to the person it makes no sense. One can guarantee after some time the message means something positive. Never be afraid in your mediumship to give what you get, it can always be passed on so as not to give hurt to others. This is taking personal responsibility.

During one of my sittings I was shown a cup and I saw weighing of sugar; to my generation this can hold memories but to the younger people it seems to have no meaning. It is often the small piece of evidence that proves who and what the person is and the positive proof of survival. In fact, the sitter's mother was a manageress in a co-operative grocery department who used to weigh the sugar. She was very proud of it and working at the co-op had been a family tradition from her grandfather onwards, who had been an undertaker at the co-op in the past.

Sometimes during a reading I wonder if I am potty, then my friends of the Spirit world talk to me of something and I have to learn the lesson, all over again, to trust in their wisdom.

There are times when I think to myself, why battle on trying to work for Spirit world? Then I weigh up all the bad bits of self-doubt and I know that as long as there is breath in my body, I will continue to work for Spirit. I know, as all mediums will tell you, mediumship spares no holds, it seems that every day brings more and more tests, to make you wonder about your strength to go on. A few sittings sometimes can seem hard, then you get the special one that brings immense joy to the sitter, when proof of survival is so strong, and for that second your heart sings, for you have done the task allotted to you.

No medium, no matter how famous or how early in life, must ever lose track that it is the Spirit who communicates. Without the bond there is no good connection with Spirit. There are many bad mediums trying to con or fool people. At the end they must remember Spirit understands everything and will soon sort them out. Also, all mediums one day will be in Spirit and will see the point from the other side.

ON ONE OF MY JAUNTS

I had been working late at a party booking with a friend and we were both booked to work about a hundred and fifty miles away the next evening. We decided to travel down after the party booking and then when we had had enough we planned to sleep in the transit van that we were travelling in. Well, this we did; we travelled some way and then when we were both rather tired we looked for a quiet spot to lay our heads.

I must admit we had no idea where we were, we just laid the bed down and soon we were sound asleep. When I awoke about 2 o'clock in the morning, my friend Fiona was snoring her head off. I was about to thump her and tell her to shut up when I heard a lorry stop. Naturally I was nosy and peered out of the window. A man ran down the side of the van and proceeded to spend a penny at great speed.

Then my friend gave a most horrendous snore, and the poor man could not pull his pants around him quick enough. He ran back to his lorry. Next morning we awoke, and started to put the bed back, ready to be on our way again. I began to tell Fiona about the night before, and we both enjoyed the laugh. As we got out of the van we could not believe our eyes, of all the places to park we were in the gates of a churchyard. I felt this was carrying it a bit too far.

We continued our journey and duly arrived at our destination. As we started to talk to our host she started to tell us of her experiences the night before. She said that she had got up in the early hours of the morning to go to the bathroom and on going back into her bedroom she was met by a number of Spirits. Having the same understanding as us, it did not bother her. The Spirits were telling her how they had passed, and she asked them to leave her room as she needed her sleep. This they did. She came to the conclusion that as we had shared their resting place, they would share hers!!

DON'T LIKE TAXIS

I had had a particularly bad day and I felt very tired and decided I was going to have a break. As anyone who is a medium will understand, sometimes tiredness can hit you very quickly and emotions build up, for you are sensitive to other people's grief and hurt and you cannot always pull the blind down! I had just returned from a long working day and previously had flown two days before, so my schedule had left me feeling very weary. I had a telephone call, about which I must admit two parts of me said, "Ignore it, don't answer it," but the conscious in me said, "Answer it," and thank God I did!

It was a very distraught lady. I felt her hurt and her sadness and my heart turned over. She said, "Please, please, please see me." So I told her I would see her that evening and she came to visit me. She asked me if I had heard about the accident, to which I replied, "What accident?" She said, "Oh, it happened two weeks ago," to which I said that I did not have time to read the papers and that very rarely do I have time to discuss them. She said she felt as though the world had ended for her and she started to cry. And as she began to cry, I sensed a young man come in. I could have sat and cried with her, which would not be very professional of me, but I felt her heartache, and this young man stood with his arms around her. He said he was her son, her only son, her pride and joy. He said he had a sister but he lived at home with his mum and dad, and promptly turned to her and said, "Eh, what's my dad doing sitting out in that car – tell him to come in." His mum said, "He did not like to, he thought it was a cheek!" So another cup was brought out, another seat set up and we carried on.

And as this gentleman, the boy's father, bit back the tears, he poured his heart out. The young lad of Spirit said to me that he had decided he would go for a ride that night. He had said to them that he would not be long. So what had he done – he had taken his motorbike out and gone for a spin. He should never have been where he was, which was often the case, and as he pulled out from the end of the road a taxi had come from nowhere and they had collided. He said that he had known nothing about it. The doctors told his mum he was still alive when he got to the hospital but he had known nothing about it. He was in the world of Spirit. He said he felt nothing, he felt no pain. He said that one of his mates was waiting for him and he then went on to talk about his funeral. He said that they had to leave the doors open because there were so many people there. He was quite a keep fit enthusiast and now his mates were arguing about who would carry him. His passing had brought such grief, such sorrow, but he was adamant that he would be with them on his birthday. I did not understand this at the time but all he kept saying was, "Happy New Year Mum, Happy New Year. I am fine. I would not have wanted to live to be a cripple, which I would have been, and I know what you said the other night when you said, 'I would look after him, no matter how much of a cripple he was, I just want my boy'. He then went on, "I could not be a cripple, mam, I want to be free, I can be anywhere and do anything I want to do now," and then he was laughing over boyish jokes and talking about his mates. My young friend has been to see me many times since; his smile is wonderful, his grin infectious and his love beyond all measure.

ONE OF MY PRIVATE SITTINGS

During one of my private sittings, long before the public sitting started, I sensed and felt the closeness of a spirit lady. She appeared quite faintly and rather hazy, so I knew that she was indeed a very new spirit. I had this overwhelming scent of roses and she kept saying to me, "Rose is here, listen, Rose is here, my sister is bringing me roses this afternoon. Tell her I prefer the yellow ones." This seemed a little strange and I could not get my head around it but I thought, never mind, it would all evolve.

The lady for the sitting duly arrived and for some reason I felt I needed to make her a cup of tea. As I put the cups on the table I distinctly was told from Spirit, "Three sugars please," (and I thought I liked sugar!) but obviously it was for the client. As the sitting progressed, my client's mother came forward and said how happy she was to be with her daughter in Spirit, and they were having a good natter together. Then I proceeded to tell my client about my early visitor. Suddenly it all became very clear, for the client was going to see her sister that afternoon to say her goodbyes; she had been laid out that morning and the client had been debating what colour of rose to give her —she said her sister's name was Rose and her favourite perfume, rose perfume. So instead of the red rose, she was able to know it was to be the yellow rose. My client had said, because of the circumstances, she did not know if she could keep her appointment but had felt a great need to come – for Spirit had relayed their thoughts to her – and now she knew the reason why.

GRUESOME TIMES – DURING A PRIVATE READING

One day a lady came to see me, who we will call Pam. Now Pam was in a terrible state, very, very upset, confused and frightened. She had just lost her mother. We all associate our mothers with love and kindness but this was not the case with Pam. Her mother never really wanted her and had no hesitation in telling her, and all her life Pam had felt inferior to her mother. And yet at the end of her mother's life she questioned, "What have I done? Why did she dislike me?" Pam had come to seek my help because she was feeling her mother's presence all the time and it was not pleasant. Her mother had never wanted to talk to her when she was alive, so Pam was upset that this was happening now.

Her mother had been mean all her life and was even mean at the end. In fact her mother disliked all girls intensely, so only the brother was favoured. As we were talking I felt the mother's presence very strongly and even at this point, she was asking about her money, her jewellery, her handbag. She had been killed in a head-on car accident and because of the circumstances only one person had identified her, for it was not a pleasant sight but a very distressing one. It seemed to me that the lady in question was continually clenching her hand and I wondered why. When I asked her what was the matter with her hand, she said that she had lost her hand during the car crash and strangely, her hand had not been found, neither had her handbag. She said they were still in the car, deeply embedded in the engine, and that the car was still under police supervision.

I felt this woman's antagonism and her hostility was directed towards everybody, and I knew that she had many lessons to learn on the other side in the Spirit world. I asked Pam, the young lady, if the car had been thoroughly investigated and her reaction was, "Well, I have not seen it, neither has my brother, as there is still the inquest to take place." I said, "Well, your mother is saying to me that her handbag and her hand are still in the car, embedded in the engine. In her handbag, true to her character, she carried all her jewellery, didn't she?" Pam went ashen and quietly nodded. This was probably the reason her mother seemed forever around her, maybe taunting and causing such hurt. I think after a time of talking through the problem Pam seemed happier, with the strong conviction that she must ask the police to examine the car further. She then said that she would come back and tell me what they found, but I knew what they would find, even though it had been missed before.

Two days later I received a telephone call. Yes, the hand and the handbag were squashed deep in the engine of the car. I checked on Pam later on again in the week, and the difficult visits from her mother had stopped. Now she just wished to try to put her life back into perspective. Where there had previously been anger, there was now only pity, for her mother had much to learn.

NEW YEAR HOLIDAY

My husband John and I went away on holiday for the New Year. We both like to dance but now that our bones are stiffening up with age, we don't move as well as we used to, but still enjoy the music.

On this New Year's Eve we were naturally late going to bed, and as we walked along the corridor I heard three young men talking, but it was not in English. It appeared to be Polish. I looked at them and thought, "Wow, what are they doing in here because they are not English – perhaps they have been to a fancy dress party?" They were not dressed as soldiers of today but as soldiers of the last war. As I followed John into the bedroom, one young man turned and looked at me strangely, as much to say, "What are you doing here and who are you? Weird woman!" It seemed as though they were looking for somewhere, and I was about to ask them if they needed any help, when they just disappeared. No trace of them was left. Then it dawned on me, they were Spirits. When I went back into the bedroom and told John what had happened, I do believe he wondered how many 'spirits' I had consumed!

The next day, as we were about to check out of the hotel, one of the young male staff said to me (he knew who I was), "Have you seen anything strange while you have been at the hotel?" To this I replied, "Yes. I saw a group of young soldiers," and told him the story. He said, "They always show themselves to someone when the hotel is full, they like company! They were billeted here in the last war and died under tragic circumstances." The young man who was an under manager promised that on my next visit there he would also take me into the cellars, which are well known for their Spirit 'guests', not the liquid sort. So when I go back, I will visit where the Spirits are, but sadly not in the bottles!

PAUL

Paul lived not far from me. He was blessed with a very loving family and I loved him dearly; he was no angel, but a normal teenager. He liked to be one of the boys, and like most boys, he liked the girls. But he had a very soft heart. He adored his niece who was an invalid, only four years old. On the particular day in question, Paul had been invited to his niece's birthday party and he was due to go but like most lads, he decided he would go out with his mates first, and out of character he went to a place which was not his usual haunt.

He went to a lake and for some reason, proceeded with two other mates to row up the lake. They had no life jackets, and like most young men, they took many things as a joke. They must have been fooling around in the boat for the boat overturned. Whether the boat struck his head was debatable but Paul was drowned. When his sister came to visit me she came for confirmation of how he had died and why he was there, because it was a mystery to the family and there was much secrecy from his mates.

He promptly came 'in', laughing and joking at her all the time and he kept poking her in the shoulder, which was apparently his usual trick. He said he was sorry for missing his niece's birthday party and for spoiling it for them all, and called himself a 'prat', but he had wanted to be one of the boys. He said that he had gone overboard and in the confusion had bumped his head. When he was finally found, he had been dead for some time, for the boys in their panic were slow to report the accident. He then went on to say that only one of his shoes had been found and that his niece's present, which was with him at the time of his death, was not found either. He was more upset and cross with that than anything else.

He then continued to tell me about his bedroom and about his 'sweaty feet', and how he did not like his bedroom being made into a shrine. He showed me what was in the top drawer of his dressing table: a key ring, some photos and young men's 'things'. He said he did not know anything really about the accident and the first thing he knew was that he was cold and that everyone had all been looking for him. He said it was his birthday in a few weeks' time, and went on to say that his niece had joined him in Spirit a week after passing, and that now they lay side by side. He brought me a bunch of flowers, a bunch of jasmine, which held extra proof of survival, to give to his sister. This young man still comes and talks to me for he is a great guy, both in Spirit and as a loving brother and son to his earth family.

SPIRITS HELP

Some time ago I was asked to go to a house to prepare for a funeral service. We sat and talked a while and after a couple of cups of tea and general chit-chat, the business at hand had to be spoken of. The lady of the house was distressed, for it was her husband that we were to bury and his personal documents could not be found – the birth and marriage certificates. As anyone knows, at times like this it is sad enough to try to come to terms with the loss of someone, without the added worries of formalities. She said she had searched high and low for these documents and could only presume they had been left behind in the last move. This was causing many problems. It is strange how two certificates can say so much and yet in words, say so little.

The wife of the deceased decided again to put the kettle on. The formalities of the funeral had been settled but we could go no further at that time because of the legal papers. I was sitting on my own in the lounge and as usual was having a conversation with Spirit. I can remember very clearly saying, "Where on earth are those documents?" and clear as clear I heard a voice saying, "If only they would open their bloody eyes, they would know where they are. They are in the back bedroom under the small bed, in a biscuit tin, covered in dust." And again I heard a 'stomp, stomp' and nothing else. So when mine host came in I said to her, "I understand you have a back bedroom, a single bed, and under the bed is a biscuit tin. You will find the documents in there." She replied, "Phew, I don't think so, I haven't looked under that bed for ages." Then I heard a laugh from the Spirit realms. "Too bloody true!" I heard a voice say, "hence the dust!" She went upstairs, came down with a red face to say, "Well, nothing escaped him in life and nothing escaped him in death – here's the bloody tin!" and the documents were indeed inside.

So don't be frightened to ask Spirit – but don't be surprised how you receive the answer. I returned home, laughing to myself all the way and thinking, why didn't she clean under the bed!

DEMONSTRATION IN A MORGUE

Some time ago I did a demonstration in a room I haven't worked in before; it was quite an awesome-looking place but nevertheless I went in with a smile on my face, stood there and wow, ooh, the energy! It wasn't what I normally like. I started to try and lift the energies. I began to talk to the people gathered there. They were fine but it was the atmosphere of the room that was the problem, very heavy. I looked up and to my amazement I could see rows and rows of feet, with big tags on the toes and I thought, well I've had some funny things in my time but this is it. So I questioned, I asked a Spirit, what are you trying to show me? Why are you making this so hard to work? The people were keen, it was a sell-out, and as it was for charity, a children's charity, I wanted to do the best I could for them. I knew Spirit was with me but it was the atmosphere. After a couple of minutes it didn't seem to be lifting and again I looked at these feet, and then my friend spoke in my ear and said, "My daughter, do you know where you are? Do you know why you are getting this?" I answered, no. "Look and think and inwardly digest," and of course, I realised it was the old morgue. The old city morgue and that's why the feet were there. Not a pretty sight, big ones, fat ones, thin ones, small ones, but still feet.

A little later on I again visited the same room. I now knew what I was going into and I was well prepared. And yes, I did see a couple of odd feet but it didn't affect me for I knew that I had to overcome these vibrations. I was lucky, for at that time there were a lot of healers in the audience and they also sent their loving energy. And thanks be, the evening again was a success. So you see, it pays us in this business not to be complacent, not to accept that it's going to be OK but it does pay and it always will pay to trust in the Spirit energy. They will not let you down. It is sometimes the human factor that does not listen and I can say honestly now, I don't mind working in that room, it doesn't bother me two hoots and I do know that whatever comes up in future I can raise the energies. This also happened not so very long ago.

I worked in a place in Northern Ireland, where the energies were not good; I felt a great sadness there and a great deal of heartache. As I stood on the platform, I was very much aware of a troop of young soldiers marching in, Spirit soldiers. They marched up to the front, turned, saluted and moved to the back, and the one young lad with them said, "Oi, my grandma's here, would you just tell her I'm all right?" I said, "What's your name honey?" "Pat," was all I got. So I put the word out and because of the area and because of the feeling in that area, of course no one would accept it. There were these poor young soldiers standing there; I felt sorry for them, they had made the effort to come and talk from the realms of Spirit. So I gave it out again and I said, "I will not give it again now, I only give three times and if no one can take it I move on, for there are many people who wish a message from Spirit and it is sad to waste time." The young soldiers then disappeared and at the end of the evening this old lady came up to me and she said, "You know, there was a terrible, terrible time here when a whole load of young soldiers were massacred, and my grandson was one of them, Pat," and I said, "Darling, why didn't you put your hand up? He so wanted to talk to you." And she said, "I didn't want people to know, I didn't want people to know." I thought then, what a sad thing. I cannot always bring those energies back, sometimes I can but sometimes I can't. What a shame for the young soldier who had come to say hello, and for the hopeful grandmother who had been there. Never mind, it was a lesson to be learned.

A CRY FROM THE HEART

One day I sat in the company of a colleague, basically for an ordinary sitting. We sat in silence and I tuned in and then the strangest thing happened. I felt the energies coming in so very, very strong and I felt as though the windows had been blown out, and the spirit energies with me were immense. I felt my body grow. I felt as though I was three times the size I normally am and the words of wisdom that came forth were wonderful. For while I was there I had the presence of a very strong Indian guide and he spoke of nurturing mother earth, of the cruelty to man and the need for

66

man to put back into the earth and not take the goodness away. Apparently he went on and on and he spoke for a good half hour and when the energy started to move away, it was as though part of my body went with it, the room stopped vibrating and I was back as I had been. Unfortunately I cannot remember much of what was said, that's quite normal, but the gentleman whom I sat with gave me very strong information. And to say the least, I was so amazed at the power of the Spirit. I don't think I had ever felt such power of Spirit before and I hope that I would be privileged to feel it again, for this indeed was an incident I could never forget, neither would I want to, for the power of Spirit was so special.

A very dear friend of mine, an elderly lady I can honestly say I could not admire more, is a very stalwart spiritualist. She went through a rough time when everything seemed to be going wrong. First the boiler blew up, then the cooker broke down, and then the garage door broke. She was at her wits' end, plus the fact she had personal problems to do with administration of her church work. Now she told me that in desperation she had stood in the hall and she had said, "I can not go on much longer. Where am I going to find the necessary to do all these jobs? I can't do without my heating. Can't you do something about it, Spirit?" It was a cry from the heart. Not much was thought about it after that but as my friend walked from the hall into the kitchen it seemed warmer, but she thought, "Well, perhaps it's me." I tell you this, within three-quarters of an hour, for no explained reason and no logical reason, the central heating was working and even the engineer who came the next day said he couldn't understand it. So my friend had a good little smile to herself as much to say, "Ah, Spirit works in mysterious ways."

THE OLD SCOUT SONG

During one of my talks with a client, we would usually talk about everyday things, about the weather, whatever really came to mind and then we would get down to more serious business. Now, I myself, if I am reading for someone, like to have music playing very low. I have decided it's a good energy to work with and there's not that strange silence. I also feel that it puts the client at ease. As we started to talk, I was very much aware of a Scoutmaster in the room with us. He started to sing the old scout song, 'Ging gang gooly...', and I found myself humming it. Anyway he turned and said, "Would you mind telling my girl that she's still got my scout cap? It's on top of the back bedroom wardrobe," and I thought, "Wow, right, OK," so I did so and to this she replied, "Do you know I was only looking at that yesterday and wondering whether to get rid of it? It's dad's old Scoutmaster's cap." I said, "Well, he knows you've got it so that's fair enough." And then he went on to talk about his grandson who was going a little bit off the beaten track and he said, "My girl, what he needs is discipline." He gave his name, he gave his grandson's name and he also gave the number of the house where he lived and the house where she lived; with this he turned his face and looked at one side of me and said, "Ask her about the willow tree," and at this she nearly freaked. "Oh my God," she said, "we were debating yesterday about the willow tree and whether to have it cut down or not, and I said to my husband that my dad wouldn't like it, he wouldn't like it one bit. He loved his willow tree." At this her father turned and said, "Too bloody right, I do love my willow tree and believe you me it is well rooted." When I relayed the evidence she said, "Well, we were wondering because as you know we had gales a few weeks ago, and we were not sure of the strength of the roots because the tree has been there since my mum and dad were courting." To this he replied, "And it will be there a damn sight longer and all if you leave it alone."

And to me this was a personal touch, which meant so much to her to know her dad was there with her, and then he turned and he grinned again, saying, "Tell her we don't argue up here. Your mum and me don't argue, we've got better things to do." He said,

"I was a cantankerous old fag," and I laughed. I relayed the message exactly as he gave it and she said, "Do you know that was his favourite saying, 'fag'? Not because he had a fag but it was a way he thought he was swearing politely." And all I could say to her then was, "Well, they're together and they're happy. He's told you what he thinks about the willow tree but it's your decision, and you've got to live with it. He also keeps on talking about his old house and as you know he's given me the number." She said, "Well actually, it's on the market now," and he piped up, "Well tell her, in three days' time it will be sold, and not to get disheartened, stick out for the price." So I wondered to myself, "Did they stick out for the price? Did they get the price?" The Spirit said they would and if Spirit states a fact they are not far wrong, and so I will leave that thought with you.

AMERICA

A couple of years ago I visited some very dear friends in America and the strangest thing is, they became friends through my chatting to one of them on a train, when I was going to do a church service. She had asked me where I was going and I explained. My husband was with me at that time and it was pouring with rain. I told her what I did and she was very interested. As I started to talk to her there was a gentleman I could see standing beside her. Yes, it was her father-in-law who spoke of her mother, saying she was upset and worried about them. To this my friend replied, 'It's all right now, we've sorted it out.' And as the conversation went on, we came to their stop for they were then travelling on the boat over to Ireland. My new friend didn't want to go. She would have loved to come with us all the way but they had already bought tickets for the crossing. I said, "Never mind," and gave her my address. She said, "I'll be in touch with you." I thought she would but anyway, within a week of her returning home, I had a phone call and we still keep in touch. I was invited out to their home in America and I can honestly tell you, it was the experience of a lifetime. My husband was asked to go but he didn't particularly want to travel, he's not so outgoing as I am, rather shy actually. So I went by myself and I was taken into areas I thought I would never see: the American Indian areas, the gold-panning country, everything that we dream of in England. The strangest thing was that I should be travelling at my age now doing all the things that I had dreamed about, and I often say to myself, "Why couldn't it have happened when I was younger? Why?" But I know now why it couldn't. I had to know a lot more about life and I certainly have learnt a lot by listening to the Spirit. I am going to America again shortly and this again is a pleasure trip to visit a colleague who lives in the Black Mountains. I am so looking forward to communing with Spirit in a nature way, and I do believe that the Indian who once appeared to me a long time ago will come again for I feel his presence very strongly.

A SPECIAL BUDGIE

During a church service recently, while I was standing there I happened to hear budgies singing or squawking, whatever you like to say. It was so distinct, and then in my mind's eye I saw a beautiful green budgie fly across the room and sit on a lady's shoulder. Obviously she wasn't aware of this but to me it was very clear. Then the budgie started to talk, very strangely. He was saying, "Shut that bloody door," and he said it three times, which made me smile. Then he turned round and said, "Who loves ya, baby?" again a joy to hear. So obviously I went to the lady and I said to her, "You've got a very special friend with you, a budgerigar," and the tears fell down her face immediately. I said, "Oh dear, he's talking to you," and I explained what he had said and again she cried. I thought, you know, this is a budgie we're talking about, even though I know you can love an animal. Then she said, "That is the most wonderful thing I could hear, because this morning we buried our Joey in the front garden. We got up and he was dead in the cage and now I know he will not leave me, I know he's around." How wonderful to think of an animal in touch, a supposedly dumb animal – I say supposedly for I do not believe animals are dumb." The husband turned and it flew away, for she had acknowledged the message, and I know she will hear that bird call her. It came to give her love and proof of the everlasting in the animal kingdom.

A FEW BOB

Sometime ago during the course of a demonstration, I looked up and I saw a gentleman walk in, prop himself against the door and listen to what I was talking about. I looked at him and there was something strange. Yes, I could see him but it was if he was glowing. I thought it was the sun shining on him but it wasn't, for this gentleman was Spirit. I heard him call and say, "My missus is here, her name is Vera. She's come because she is curious, too damn curious. Now I'm going to stop and make her think. Tell her that it's Arthur here. Tell her it's her old man, I was caretaker of this building many years ago." He then proceeded to talk to me of Spirit saying how long he had been in Spirit and he started to fumble in a pocket and I thought, this is strange. What's he doing? And believe it or not, he was jangling coins about as he used to do regularly. He said, "And tell her I heard what she said at my funeral. Tell her I heard her say, 'He will not be happy unless he's got a few bob in his pocket,'" and with that the lady, his good lady, roared with laughter and everybody laughed with her, for he had his few bob in his pocket and he was a happy man, just keeping an eye on her. Off he went whistling, whistling between his teeth saying, "That'll make her think!" Which it certainly did.

COMFORT TO A WIFE

It is my policy to try to do quite a lot of charity demos and at one particular one I was working with a good friend of mine. We often worked together as a team and all seemed to be going very well. Immediately I tuned in I heard a young man say to me, "My wife's over there. Tell her I've been with her all day. Tell her, yes, I like the dress she bought for the little 'un and tell her that in her purse she has a lucky charm that I had. Ask her to open her purse up and show it to you, it's a St Christopher." So I relayed the message to the young lady and indeed it was her husband, who kept on saying, "I'm sorry, I'm sorry for the hurt I caused her. I'm sorry for not seeing sense but just tell her more than anything, I'm all right. I'm with God, I'm not being punished for being weak and it is wonderful up here but I do miss them, yes. I want her to get on with her own life now, for she has a long life ahead of her. Look after my baby. I'm all right. Oh, and incidentally, I hung myself."

I could feel the emotion with him. I could feel and see the emotion with his wife and she said, "I came tonight with an open mind. I did not believe, but no one could possibly know that today I bought a new dress for our little girl." And yes, she turned her purse out and there was a lucky charm. There wasn't much money in the purse so this girl had obviously had to watch her pennies to be able to come, and my heart went out to her. He told her his name, he also mentioned what she had given him in his coffin, the most beautiful red rose, because he said he had the rose with him. He then turned and said, "It's her birthday in a few weeks' time and tell her that I do love her. I'm sorry I hurt her and I will always be around. I'll always be around if she needs me but she has to get on with her own life." And he told me his birth date and he himself was only twenty-four. What a waste of life. It is a great pity because life is so precious and it is a gift of God, but God does not punish those who are weak, for our God, I strongly believe and I know, is a loving God and there is enough love within the Spirit world for everyone.

FOOLED YOU

It was a winter's evening and I was returning from a neighbouring church. As my friend was driving along the road I suddenly saw someone move in front of us. She also saw them and she braked hard, leaving us both shaken. We knew we hadn't hit whoever it was but it was certainly a near one. We got out of the car and walked up the road, but there was nobody around. We couldn't believe what we were seeing, there was nobody. There was nowhere this person could have gone. Then we really started to panic. I mean, we all hear of hit and run drivers but we certainly weren't running, we were looking, but there was no one in sight. Then I heard a voice say, "I've just come to look at the flowers," and my heart turned over. A few yards ahead of us were flowers by the roadside in memory of a young lad who had been knocked down on that corner. We got back in the car and I must admit I felt fright, fear, I don't know, we were very shaken. Now whenever I pass that spot, I think to myself, my, that lad loved flowers. I'm not saying he's earthbound, he's not, but curiosity sometimes gets the better of us even in Spirit and we come back and have another look. He's at peace, that I do know. But I'm not the only one who has seen him on that stretch of road. My driver saw him but many other people have also and that indeed is proof of survival.

PREVIOUS LIFE

A general topic of conversation is previous lives. Everyone can draw his or her own conclusion, and I have mine. During the course of your life on earth, there are many things that happen to you, which make you stop and say, "How do I know that place? Why is it so familiar? I feel I've been there before, I've done this, I've done that…" And then you start to try and think logically. Such a thing happened to me about twenty-odd years ago. We had not long moved to where we live now and I was walking down the road, quite slowly. I reached the corner and yet I saw myself on the opposite side of the road, and I saw a horse and cart. I saw myself on the floor and in my heart of hearts, I knew it was me but not the 'now' me, but the 'past' me.

What I could see appeared to be a milk cart pulled by a horse, with milk churns in the back of it. At that minute I thought I saw myself, not dressed as I would be today, but with a long black skirt and boot-type shoes. It was an old me and I must confess, shudders ran up and down my spine. Within a second of seeing it I was transported back to the present time. I tried to find out about the past of that particular road and I was told that it was a common thing years ago to see some carts being pulled like that, and for milk churns to be carried on the back. I never ever found out why they should show myself, but I do know this: of all the times of living in that village, I never did like that corner and I would walk if possible another quarter of a mile to avoid that area. Time I know would not repeat itself but it was there, the memory.

TWIN SISTER

I received a telegram call on a Saturday morning; it was from a gentleman who was very upset and very concerned. He asked me if I would be able to help his wife and I thought I would see what I could do, so he came to see me. My so-called private sittings are individual and personal, but very rarely do I charge because I feel this is a way of repaying peace of mind for all those years ago when I had nothing. I do not do many private sittings now for it takes so much energy, and I prefer to go into the larger groups to people who don't know and people who need to know, that there is life after death.

This particular lady who came to see me looked so tired. She sat in the chair and had a cup of tea, and she started to cry. She had been so overwrought for she was having terrible nightmares, horrific nightmares of drowning and she said, "I can feel the water going over my head, I can feel myself going down, I can feel all these things and I am so frightened, so frightened of being on my own, so frightened of anything over my face and I don't understand. It's just happened inside the last three months." I took my thoughts to the Spirit and asked, "Can you shine any light on this? Will you help me?" And immediately I sensed a young girl in the room with us. She said her name was Jean and she went up to the lady and put her hand on her shoulder. I knew this woman was conscious of her, I could see the way her shoulders moved and I asked Jean, "Who are you?" She answered, "I am her sister, that's my sister you're talking to. I've come to say hello. I have been trying to call her for weeks but she won't listen. I just want to say that I'm all right, and not to worry, I'm fine. I so like the new bedroom curtains and I love the basket in the bathroom." I said, "Thank you, Jean. Let's see what your sister has to say."

I relayed all this to the lady and I said, "You have a sister in the Spirit world," and she gasped and put her hand to her mouth straight away. "Oh yes," she said, and I think she was telling me her sister went very tragically, that she was drowned. "Yes," she said, "but I have never acknowledged it even though I know it to be a fact. She fell in a lock by the canal." Again her sister said, "But I'm all right, I'm fine." But then I started to talk to the lady and I said, "It's your sister who's been trying to say hello to you, and she's done it the way she knows, like telling you the way she passed. You know about that but you do not know much about her." And so the conversation went on. The lady had had a twin sister and they had both been playing together, when the twin who was drowned had wandered off and obviously had died. But my friend's parents did not talk very freely about it, so Jean had a great deal of difficulty in being acknowledged. Therefore she solved it in the way she thought she would get attention by giving the feeling of how she died with the water, to which my friend said, "Oh, I never thought of that."

I said, "She is your twin, so you are of the same blood and therefore your sensitivity is very highly linked. Don't worry, she probably won't give you that feeling again now you have acknowledged her." Then I went on to say that her sister loved the curtains in the bedroom, to which my friend replied, "I only put them up three days ago," and I thought again that was lovely. She then spoke about the bathroom stool, which apparently had come from her parents' house. When she and her sister were very little, they used to squabble who would sit on the stool. It is what we call a Lloyd Loom stool and in this day and age it has come back into its own fashion. I never heard any more from the lady or her husband so I know she's quite happy, and I know she is no longer afraid. I am sure she knows that she is loved by her sister, Jean, in the Spirit world.

KEEP IN TOUCH

Recently I telephoned a friend. We hadn't spoken for close on two years or maybe longer, and I had lost her address. For a long time I could never seem to find it and then from nowhere appeared this letter on my table; yes, it was my friend's address, so promptly I rang and she was just as flabbergasted as I was that I had found the letter. She said I had been on her mind the day before and two or three times she had wondered if she would ever she would see me again or speak to me. However the strangest thing of all is that the week before, she had moved house and picked up a photo of us together. Not only that, because she had changed her house I would never have found the address anyway, but she had been fortunate enough to take the same phone number with her. And as strange as it seems, thought is very important. So now we are going to resume our friendship, which has never been broken but we are going to bring it back together, because we can now contact each other. Spirit moves in strange ways because she had been thinking so hard how to find me or me to find her, and she had been speaking about me the day before. I say with all honesty, think, be positive and all will work well.

JUST TO SAY HELLO

There is a lot spoken about Spirits that hang around, and there is a lot spoken about people who are disturbed by Spirits; but you know, very often and too often people ask a trained medium to help to move the Spirits on, back into the realms of night. Now my policy is that, before I could consider anything so extreme, is to ask whether there's any Spirit energy out there. There's no harm in that, but they've usually come because they want to be acknowledged and are eager to communicate. Perhaps they have a message and have taken the trouble to come forward. Very often if anyone feels or senses something, it is because the Spirit has come with love, and it takes energy for a Spirit to make ccntact. I know if I was up there I wouldn't waste my energy if I didn't want to come, so basically and truthfully, if the Spirit talks to you it is because of the love it has for you, the energy and the vibration.

You can walk in many paths of light and you can walk in many ways but there are times when you also must challenge. Most Spirits are good but there are one or two that are not so good, so then you use the law of challenge: Are you in the light? Are you in the light? Are you in the light? If you feel in your heart there is no positive yes, then you challenge again and then it's time to ask them to go to the light. Sometimes when you feel that they've caught some of the light, you have to ask again, "What do you want to say? What do you want to do? Tell me and I will help you." And at other times, if there has been a tragic setback, or a passing that shouldn't be, you must be able to say, "I will help you. All is well," and all will be well.

OUR CHURCH CHILDREN

The church, which I am a president of, is in a very small building, really too small, but the feeling in there is a loving feeling. We are very blessed for we seem to have a lot of Spirit children in our church and very often if I go there on my own and I open the door, I can hear the children laughing and that is incredible.

Last Christmas, like most churches, we had a Christmas tree and it was beautiful. The theme was lovely, and at the Christmas carol service we had a wonderful time. Of course there was a buffet afterwards and everybody could feel the love that was within. On that particular day on entering the church, I set the table up. My friend was working with me, when we heard the most amazing giggle that you could possibly imagine, and it was gorgeous. We could hear children laughing, and thought some little ones were upstairs, yet we knew it was not possible, and of course, when we went upstairs there was no one there. As I turned to go down the stairs, I distinctly heard a little voice call, "Hello." We put the carols on and we had them singing with us, which was love within the church.

Well, we decided it was time for a cup of tea and we sat down to have our drinks but what happened? The Christmas lights, which had been off, came on, then they went off and on, and believe you me, there was no electricity problem, just the energy of Spirit. The day after that we had a service at that church, and I could see the children, all shapes and sizes, and they were happy to be there. Since that day we regularly hear the Spirit children playing, and to me that is lovely and comforting.

Another day when I arrived at the church, I was, as often happens, the only one there, and I unlocked the door and walked into the church area. I felt as though I was being watched as indeed I was. I looked across the room and in the corner sat an old lady who smiled at me. I could not understand how on earth she had got in without me seeing her. My first reaction was, "Oh goodness, she has been in here all night. Is she all right?" I walked up to her and heard her say, "You are doing a good job, I understand that. Look after yourself dear."

Next second she was gone. I felt very privileged that she had come forward. At that time it seemed as though I had mega problems to deal with, such as church business, but I felt so much better for her words of comfort.

I described this lady to a committee member of long standing, who said it was the church's first founder president who had been in Spirit for many years.

HAPPY BIRTHDAY MUMMY

During an evening clairvoyance recently I saw the presence of three children, but they were not the church children that I saw, these were three other children, all sitting down the middle of the room, laughing. One, who had been drowned in the bath, told me she had come to talk to her mummy's friend. "It was only a little water," she said, "I hit the back of my head and now I'm with God and the angels and the fairies," and she was quite happy about it and giggling all the time. "But tell my mummy's friend, she's sat over there, the lady with the jacket on. Tell her it's my mummy's birthday next week and happy birthday from me." And on giving the message I was told yes, the lady's friend's daughter was drowned in the bath, an accident, and yes, there was a party around. So you see Spirit knows what's going on, there is nothing to worry about because God looks after all of His children. Yes, I have spoken to many famous people and it would be wrong to relate any of the information, but I can say this, no matter if you have got millions or pennies, there is a time when everyone needs to know that their loved ones in Spirit are around them.

CHILLIES AND FREESIAS

It was a Monday morning and I was very conscious of a lazy feeling around me. I didn't feel I wanted to do anything, but just felt bone idle I suppose. Anyway, about 11 o'clock I was sat on the settee quite happily when lo and behold, I closed my eyes, then wow! Immediately I felt the presence of a soldier in front of me; he stood there tapping his heel and he said, "Hello young 'un. What are you doing? You should be out and about," and I thought, who's this in my front room? He then went on to talk to me about planting seeds. I thought, what's the man on about, an army soldier planting seeds? He went on to say, "Plant them deep girl, they're bound to come up all right if you do and don't forget to water them either." I thought, this is going a bit far, I'm lazy enough, why should I worry about seeds? And then he went on to talk to me about himself. He said, "Huh, my name's George, George Williams, I thought I'd come up and talk to you." I thought, what a strange way to do this, and then he went on to talk about how he used to live not far from where I lived as a child. This was getting interesting.

He knew more than that, for he said, "I'm related to you, do you know that?" This man amazed me. "I'm all right, I've got my lad with me and I've got so-and-so," and he went through all the names of his family. Then he said, "Well you're right what you said." This was getting more complicated. He said, "She does like freesias." And then it dawned on me, this man was the father of my uncle, and I had recently been talking to my own son about how my aunt loved freesias. I said, "Well, OK." No sooner had I acknowledged who he was, than he went. I wondered why he had come, but anyway the day wore on and I wasn't feeling so lazy, when the phone rang. It was my other son. "Oh mum," he said, "I'm off down to Kiddie, do you want a ride? I could pick you up on the way through." Strange as strange, but I said, "OK then, yes fine." It's about one hundred and twenty miles, and I thought this must be leading up to something, 'cos my aunty, and my parents are buried in Kidderminster. I thought that must be it, I will go to their graves and clean them up.

So off we went. My son dropped me not far from the cemetery and arranged a point for picking me up, and I walked on with the flowers I had bought en route. I had a bunch of freesias, some bulbs and a trowel I had already got with me, and then some carnations and some chillies also. Now if you don't know what chillies are, it's a Midlands' word for wallflowers, they're very pretty flowers and I love them. Anyway, to get to my mum and dad's grave I have to pass my aunt's grave, and buried with my aunt are my gran and my granddad. Now my uncle isn't buried in that grave because he was cremated, as he wished. So I thought, well, I'll do this grave first.

I was on my knees with the trowel planting some bulbs when I heard a voice saying, "Plant them deep, don't want the rain washing them away," and I said, "OK, you've got your way mate, I'm here," so that's how it went. And then I heard a little voice saying, "You know dear, I love the chillies." It was my gran's voice. I even get emotional to think about it. And so there were freesias put on the grave as well as chillies, and it looked a rare sight; so you see, Spirits had got their own way. Then I walked a bit further on to attend to my mum and dad's grave, and I did just the same routine there. But what happened? I slipped, and it's not a pretty sight when your legs are in the air and your bum hits the ground. I distinctly heard my mother say, "Girl, you're arse over tit again," which of course is a Midlands' saying for 'on your bum'. This ended a very strange day, so since I had woken up feeling lazy, I had travelled one hundred and twenty miles there and back, bruised my bum and was now back in my own home and my own bed.

GHOST

Some days are strange
My glasses disappear
My keys cannot be found
My purse is not where I left it
The cotton rolls on the ground
The doorbell rings no one is around.

Who hid my letter I put ready to post?
It must have been my friendly Ghost
I know he means me no harm
Of this I have no doubt
It is his way of saying he is about.

When next he calls
It would be easier for me if he would shout
Not move my things about
Never fear my friend Ghost
I wish not to shut you out
If you are happy to visit me
I am happy with your company my friendly Ghost.

A DEAREST WISH

On one of my visits away, a lady came to see me who later became
quite a good friend, and still is. As she sat talking to me I was aware
of a very elderly lady behind her. This I knew to be her great-
grandmother, and she was smiling and was quite happy. I started
the young lady in question talking and her great-granny butted in
mighty quickly. "Eh, she said, ask her what her desire is, ask her
what her biggest hope is and tell her, it's going to happen in
September. She is going to be very, very busy, not once but twice,

two for the price of one." I thought, wow, what's this? I did what I was told, and asked the young lady, "What is your dearest wish, your dearest desire?" She looked at me rather sadly and said, "No, I will never have that, that is not meant to be but I have a wonderful husband and I must be grateful." I said, "You know, I've got your great-gran here and she's telling me you will get your dearest desire, you will get your dearest wish and it will be not once but twice." The young lady smiled and I think she thought I was mad, for this particular lady had very serious kidney problems and her dearest wish was for children.

Anyway we talked quite a bit and time went on. When she went I said, "Remember what your nana has said." Seven weeks later I had a phone call, and it was from the young lady. She said, "I can't believe it, I'm pregnant, how did it happen?" and I said, "Well, as someone once said to me, 'God knows best.'" "But," she said, "I was told I would never have a child." I replied, "No, I don't think you are going to have one, lovey, I think you are going to have two," and then she really started to howl with laughter. "Well," she told me, "I'm off for a scan in another two weeks because of my complications, let's wait and see." Two weeks later the phone rang again, and amid laughter she said, "Margaret, are you a witch?" I answered, "No, not a witch," but there was much humour. She went on to say, 'It's twins and they told me it's going to be a difficult pregnancy, which I understand, but God willing it will be all right." I said to her, "Your great-gran said it was going to be all right, trust in the Spirit world."

All through the pregnancy she kept me informed of her progress. Yes, it was difficult, and there were times when she had to have much rest, but I was delighted when I received the news that she had had twin sons. She is delighted, her husband is over the moon, the family are delighted and great-grandma is smiling as I am recording this incident. Who can say what is around the corner when nothing escapes our loved ones in Spirit?

I was asked to do a sitting for a lady, but I wasn't quite sure; something was bothering me, I didn't know what, and my head doorkeeper (as we call my protecting guide), nodded and said, "Yes, carry on with it, carry on with it. It is all right." So I did, and as this lady came in and sat down I could feel the anxiety around her. She was indeed a troubled soul, but the strangest thing of all was that I wasn't getting my usual contact with the Spirit world. I then came to realise that they were there but they weren't talking to me, until I said to her, "I don't think this is a normal sitting dear. There is something here I am not understanding, it must be me, the Spirit World are here laughing and holding out their hands to say hello, but they are not talking to me," and to this she replied, "I did not expect them to, I did not expect them to."

Then I heard very firmly my special helper, saying to me, "Tell her about the other side, tell her about the love that is with us and the joy that we have to offer for she is afraid, she is very, very afraid." I said right, so I carried on talking and told how I had died as a young person, gone into the Spirit World, met my son and my grandmother, and felt the wonders of the Spirit world. I described the feeling of being loved, the feeling of warmth and calm, the feeling of peace, of no fear, no aches and pains. As I was talking to her a tear slid down her face and she said, "You know that's the reason I have come, don't you?" and I did, for my sitter had a very limited time of earth span available to her. She just needed to hear somebody say that it's OK, she needed to know from someone who has seen the other side.

We started to talk of many things after that, for she said she didn't really know why she had come to me, or how she had found me, but she said that three times in one day she had heard my name mentioned by different avenues of thought. Three times she was drawn to find me, and the day previously she had spoken to a friend of mine, who had no idea of her situation, but who had said roughly what I do and who I am; and that's how the sitting came about. Strangely enough I had decided at that point that I needed to rest and would not do any sittings, for as I said before it takes a lot of energy, a lot of strength and concentration. Very often I do not charge anything for my sittings for I remember the old way, when I had nothing, and what was done for me. But with this lady, despite my deciding 'no', the spirit had intervened and said 'yes'.

She left me with a smile on her face and I knew I would never see her again. As she walked through the door I thanked God, for God in his wisdom and the Spirit world for allowing me to relate what happened to me, and the comfort that I know is in the Spirit world. I heard a week later she had passed. To my surprise two or three weeks after that there was a letter through my door. I didn't recognise the envelope. I opened it and inside was a letter from the lady who had passed. Very briefly, very much to the point, she said in her letter, "Dear Margaret, I don't know when or how the Spirit put me with you but it was because my prayers were being answered. You gave me hope of life eternal. You gave me thoughts of the good things to come and as I write this letter it will probably be the last letter I will ever write. But please remember this, I thank you, I thank God and I thank Spirit for giving me the strength to face the last few weeks."

A LESSON OF LIFE

It was a Saturday morning, a time I like to think is my own, but it is not always so. I had an urgent phone call from a friend of mine asking if I would do her a favour, which to me means seeing somebody. I thought, well OK. I like to keep Saturdays free for the family, because my granddaughter once said to me, "Nan the only way to see you is to make a blinkin' appointment!" to which I must admit, she's right. Anyway, I said yes to my friend's plea, but I was told that the lady was in such a state she couldn't leave her home. Would I go to her home? I wasn't very happy about it but never mind, I took a taxi and I went to this lady's house. And as I stepped out of the taxi I heard a Spirit say very clearly, "You know, Margaret, this is another one," and I thought, "Oh, yes, another one, don't charge dear, don't charge." Strangely enough I had made up my mind anyway I wasn't going to charge.

The taxi pulled away and as I knocked on the front door I heard the crunch of wheels, which I thought was strange. When the door opened, I could see a little boy of about seven. I felt perhaps he had been riding a bike but no, he opened the door and said, "Mummy's waiting," and I said, "Oh, OK, thank you darling. You been riding your bike?" "Oh no," he said, "I've been playing with mummy's chair." I turned the corner to be faced with a wheelchair. Again I made sure I closed the door because you know what kiddies are like, but this lad seemed so, how can I say it, old for his years, yet loving and caring. I turned into the sitting room and there this lady sat in a comfortable armchair, but I could see by her aura she was not well. She smiled at me and asked if I wanted a cup of tea. I said, "No love, thanks, I'm fine." I didn't know how the cup of tea was going to come, never mind she had asked but I didn't want one anyway. So I sat down and we started to talk. We were deep in conversation and I asked her if she would allow me to contact some friends of mine who are recognised spiritual healers in the area where she lived. To which she replied, "Yes that would be lovely."

The conversation progressed and the Spirit world started to build up. As we sat there a gentleman came in who talked of the burden he had left his good lady, for he had died very tragically in a car crash. He gave positive proof of survival by talking of the things around their lives; he talked of his hopes and his fears, and then he turned around and said, "You know, I would have loved a pub," and I said, "Oh well, yes, why not?" She smiled at this because she said that even though he was not a drinker himself, he always fancied a pub. He fancied being a landlord, and suddenly we were talking, having a conversation with Spirit. He was speaking about what he had hoped for, what their plans had been, and telling her continually not to be put on by her sister. I thought, wow, careful girl, careful Margaret with what you are saying but she understood. She said, "My sister loves me but she bosses me because she worries about me," and I thought, well, that's fair enough.

Then as I was talking to this gentleman I had such a panic come to me, and then my sight suddenly went. I couldn't see a blinkin' thing! I thought, oh my God, what's happened? I could see nothing and I realised Spirit had come too close. Our friend was giving me his symptoms of how he passed, for he had passed with a cerebral haemorrhage, which took his eyesight. Now I've not got good eyesight anyway; as you probably know I have sight in one eye only, and now I thought I was going to lose my sight completely. I panicked, and then I thought, nay, you stupid woman, practise what you preach.

You teach other people how to overcome these things, so use your loaf, ask the Spirits to move back, they are too close. This I did, and as Spirit world moved further back so my sight became clearer and I could focus, but I must admit that it did knock me for six. Did I stop and think? Yes, practise what you preach, for I am always telling people that you are in control of a sitting. In other words, yes, Spirit will control if they want to come in; if they don't want to come in they won't, but you are in control of the sitting to the extent that you can say, no thank you, or yes please.

I learnt a lesson that day, which was that there have to be rules and regulations, and that there has to be positive thinking and connection, and the ability and the right to say, "Move back please." When you weigh things up Spirits do not fear the thought of anything, for they don't have to, but we do, and I learnt that day I must always be in control by accepting only what I wish to accept. Any medium will tell you when they come across any particular situation, that they have to know what they are doing and how to deal with it, for the mind can play tricks, the mind can magnify fear and you must never allow it to do that.

The sitting ended very successfully. The lady was happy for she had a decision to make about her house, and all her husband was saying to her was that he wanted the best for her and his boy. She was to use her own mind to think and to do what she wanted, and she would be receiving some good treatment in the future which would make life easier. This is what happened. This lady can now walk with two sticks and that's good. The little boy is doing very well and I say again, it's a lesson of life.

FISH AND CHIPS

On one of my tours in Ireland I found that people are quite desperate for proof of survival. They need to know that there is life after death. If anyone ever tries to convince you that fear is in Ireland, take it with a pinch of salt, because fear is everywhere, and sometimes fear is born of ignorance. I can say truthfully I have met some of the nicest people there that anyone could wish to see, for they have known much suffering in certain areas and yet the love of God is still there.

At one particular demonstration I saw a young lad, very, very clearly with his hand upon one shoulder of his mother. He was looking at her with love and yet I could sense the anger around this lady and I thought, oh dear, anger is not good to channel with but we will do what we can. As I spoke to the young man he spoke of his passing, and the strangest thing of all was that he gave me a big piece of fish. He knows I like fish and chips, who wouldn't? Me, I'm a piggy, I love my fish and chips. And then he started to talk about his passing. Yes, he said that he had been suffocated by a group of lads, and I thought to myself, what agony that mother was feeling. He then promptly showed me five pairs of feet and they were kicking left, right and centre, and I knew also that beside him was a knife, which had been used on him.

You know, it's bad enough for any mother to lose a son, but to lose a son so brutally, my heart goes out to anyone. This boy in his wisdom would not give the name of his murderers for he knew what would happen, and his final words to his mum were, "Let sleeping dogs lie, I'm all right." Again he confirmed to me that he loved the water, he loved people, but he had just got into trouble that night with the wrong crowd. He also said to me, "You know I like water, don't you? I'm a fisherman."

FAMILIES GETTING BACK TOGETHER

At another of my sittings, which I thought was funny, was with an old lady who was very keen to talk to me during a demo. She was wriggling about, moving quickly and she said, "Tell my daughter I've got me clean knickers on," and I thought, clean knickers on, right, OK, "and I wore clean knickers when I was buried." I then said, "OK honey, let's find your daughter," and she said, "She's at the back, on the back row, third in." When I looked, sitting third in on the back row was a gentleman. I thought, no, but she said, "Look, look, she's got a green cardigan on," and I looked at the other side and sure enough, there she was. I asked what her daughter's name was and she was saying something that sounded like "Isha, Isha," and I thought that Isha didn't sound right, so I said, "Tell me again, sweetheart." "Ishabel, Ishabel," and apparently it was Isobel, so I said, "Isobel, I have your mum here." This poor lady went ashen. "She's telling me you don't like to be called Isobel so what's she playing at?" She replied, "No I don't, I'm called Isa," I said, "OK, fair enough, but your mum says Isobel, so Isobel we'll call you," and she said, "That's typical of my mum, God bless her." I went on, "Well, your mum's telling me she has got her clean knickers on, and she went over with a clean pair on," and at this the lady started to smile, saying, "Well, she needed them, 'cos my mam was totally incontinent, in other words, she could cough and it could be too late." At this the old lady turned and said, "Eh, eh, eh, that's personal!" but it was banter going on between Spirit and the daughter. She turned and said to me, "Ask her about the kitchen cupboard." I thought, um right. "Your mum wants to know about what's gone wrong with the kitchen cupboard." To this the girl replied, "Bloody hell, it fell down this morning, it's my old man, he's a jack of all trades and master of none." The mother answered in Spirit, "You don't have to tell me, I've always said the same, you've got too many fingers in the pies!" The place was now in uproar because it was such genuinely family talk.

The old lady was talking about her granddaughter, because she was very concerned about her, and told me, "You know, she's having a baby." I said, "Ooh, that's nice," but she said, "Huh, another!" I replied, "Oh dear, Margaret, be careful." So I spoke to Isobel, "I understand you have got a new baby coming in the family, that's what your mother's telling me." She answered, "We only heard this morning, how does she know? But there again, nothing ever escaped her, God bless her, she was so nosey she never missed a thing." There they both were, the mother was talking to me and I was talking to her daughter, it was a conversation again with Spirit.

Out of the blue the woman said, "Ask my mother what she's got in her purse." And when I asked the old lady, "Spirit, your daughter wants to know what you have got in your purse," she answered, "I heard her, bugger all," which I thought was funny, "except my little black cat," at which the daughter squealed and said, "Nobody knows that because I have my mother's purse, and all there is in it is a little black cat that she was given, a little tiny keepsake from a gypsy." The old lady said, "That ain't all, I never turned a gypsy away, I always bought a bit of lace. Never turn a gypsy away." The daughter replied, "Too true, but didn't she use to moan afterwards, 'cos the gypsies used to talk that quickly, she couldn't understand what they said." These two would have talked on, the mother especially, who would have talked all night but unfortunately other people wanted messages so I asked her, "Please sweetheart, move aside, thank you for coming," to which she replied, "I'm here, I think I'll stop a bit." I said, "OK no problem, fine."

I still felt I was in that same row when a contact came in, a gentleman. He was laughing and talking about the copper, the copper. Now in my vocabulary a copper is a policeman. I said, "I'm looking for a young man by the name of Eamon whose dad is talking about the copper, and he is adamant about the copper." Now I had thought of a policeman, but of course it wasn't, for the young man said, "Oh I know what that is, I'm Eamon, he's my dad and we've got a backyard with an old store room. There's an old copper in there that used to be used for boiling things up, and today I started to knock the old copper out."

FRIENDS

During one of my demonstrations, I was very much drawn to two sets of people who sat side by side, and I knew that Spirits were waiting to talk to them. As I looked at them I could sense their sadness. The next thing, I heard two children laughing and playing, and there they were just at the side of me having a whale of a time, a little boy and girl. The little boy was very content to mess with the flowers on the table and he turned and he said, "Do you know that's my favourite colour? I was buried in that colour." I thought, how unusual, it was mauve. "That's my mummy and daddy there, they've come to talk," he said, and with that, the little girl pushed him aside and said, "Eh, eh, eh you, that's my mummy and daddy next to them. They've come to talk to me and I've come to talk to them!" Their childish laughter was wonderful. "I like that colour," she said, and she pointed to the pink. I said, "OK sweetheart, that's nice."

We then moved on to talk to their parents. The little girl was laughing and she was talking about her teddy bear, what was going on around her, what was going around the home and she gave positive proof of who she was. She gave her name and also said, "My mummy couldn't quite make up her mind whether to come tonight." I thought this was fair enough, then she said, "Will you tell my mummy I saw her change her jumper," for she had changed her jumper at the last minute. Then she started to talk about the house, and her bedroom. She said, "My bedroom is just the same. I don't want it, why doesn't my mummy change it to the computer room for daddy, 'cos my daddy likes computers?"

When I relayed this information she said, "My mummy and daddy and his mummy and daddy are now good friends because we both came up here to live with the angels about the same time, in fact there was just a day in between." I then turned to the little boy, who said, "I didn't go the same way as she went, oh no," he said," I went with a bang." And he started to talk about his accident. He spoke of one good thing that had come out from his passing, which was that his mummy and daddy had got two new good friends. So these people in their grief had clung together, they were not related but only related in love, and I thought from out of sadness can come hope.

At the end of the demonstration the two children were still near me, quite happy to play around. The little girl was singing to me, the little boy was riding a small trike, quite happy with that, and he was telling me about his posh clothes. He said, "Tell them about the football made of flowers, tell them." "OK," I said, but he kept on, so in the end I said, "OK darling, now I have to talk to somebody else," so what did they do? They sat cross-legged in front of me, and they stayed there all night. As the demo came to an end the little girl got up and she nudged me, "Give my mummy the pink flowers," and the boy said, "Give my mummy the purple ones." I answered, "Darling, they're not purple, they're mauve," to which he replied, "Well, give them to her because that's the colour I used to wear, that was the colour I was buried in." I said, "OK, sweetheart," and this I did, but the laughter of these children remained with me for a long time. After the evening was over I asked if both sets of parents would stop and talk to me, because there was such love there. They did so, and again instead of crying they were laughing.

MAY'S CHRISTMAS TREE

Spirits take the memories they hold dear very often into the Spirit World with them and this is how they can come back and talk to you about various things, about their lives and positive proof of evidence. As I said earlier on in the book, I had a very good friend, an old lady who I did my best to look after, May. Now May, God bless her, could be contrary. She could also be bossy, yet that was just a cover up, for she had a heart of gold. She had had a sad and lonely life and so we tried to make excuses for her. Anyway, what happened here that I would like to talk to you about is to do with May's Christmas tree.

One day we went out because May decided, yes, she would like a little electric Christmas tree that she had seen elsewhere. We found the tree she wanted, I would say, about twenty-two inches tall. It didn't have proper lights but little bulbs. Once the main bulb was lit it showed all the others up, and she loved it. She couldn't wait for it to be put up and she didn't want it taken down. When May passed I knew that the Christmas tree must stay in my house and be used, so as soon as I possibly can before Christmas, I bring out the tree to be plugged in, in all its glory. Now yes, I have an ordinary Christmas tree but things aren't right until the electric tree is up, and then I can guarantee that most mornings when I get up and go into the lounge I am met with a very familiar figure. Of course, it's May. She giggles sometimes in a childlike way and if she gets impatient she will stamp her feet, but I know it's May, as I can smell Olbas Oil. I don't know why but she had this thing about her that she had to have Olbas Oil continually on her hankie. So every morning once that tree is up I go into the lounge and there is the familiar smell.

Now, about two days before Christmas the tree would not light. It seemed as though May in her wisdom, in the Spirit World, was getting agitated. She was moving the Christmas cards and other bits and pieces around. I knew what it was, and so I had to say quite firmly, "Oi, now!" So immediately my husband had to go up to the local DIY store and get a special bulb for the centre of the tree; it's a smaller bulb than average, and so an ordinary light bulb will not fit. Fine, he came back, and put it in. Immediately the tree lit up and I again heard the familiar giggle, so all was well. She was happy and Christmas carried on. When the time comes to pack away the Christmas tree there is almost a bit of sadness in me, which may sound silly for I know May is always around me, but I remember her love of Christmas. Once again this year, God willing, the tree will come out and my house will reek with Olbas Oil; but never mind, it soon disappears and all is well.

THE NOT SO NICE SIDE

I must admit I never read papers and sadly I watch very little television. I'm one for a sob story, but films of war and violence I don't like. So it's not surprising that I had not been watching television when my husband said something about there being a panic about some little girls getting lost, but perhaps I hadn't listened carefully, I don't know. Anyway, I woke up one morning about 6 o'clock. I cannot explain the feelings I had because people would think, wow, she's flipped her lid! I couldn't settle and I was agitated, so I got up. I was pacing around, which is usual for me when I am about to work. I went into the kitchen and put the kettle on and it was almost as though my legs went from under me. It was horrible. I could feel fear, I felt sickness, I ached all over and the smell of burning was terrible yet I was cold.

94

I started to pace up and down and I then saw very clearly in my Third Eye a kind of lane, a ditch, a fence and a car in the distance. I could see a yellow number plate on the car, which was red, and I thought, this is just not making sense; and then I distinctly heard a wartime bomber go over my head. So I realised what they were showing me was an old airfield, an old runway. I heard a name mentioned, a three-syllable name and I just could not stop pacing and feeling sick. I was very agitated. When my husband got up he said, "What's the matter? What have you eaten?" I said, "Well, nothing, it's just what I'm getting." He said, "Look, have a cup of tea." But I said I didn't know what it was but it wasn't nice. Anyway while we sat down having the cup of tea he put the news on and it was announced that the little girls who had gone missing had still not been found, and the police were appealing for information. I knew then what the Spirit had shown me.

Now, I'm not a sensational person. My work to a certain point is private and no way do I wish to be labelled a crank or an opportunist but I knew I had got to say what I had felt. Now some police forces are very open to information, others I think are still sceptical of us. They gave a number on the radio, which I jotted down. I came into my workroom and I decided to phone. Now I didn't want publicity, I'm not that type of person, I just didn't want it but I could not settle until this information was given, so I rang the number and tried to withhold my own number. It didn't work, the police would not have that, so I had to give my number and spoke to somebody in what they call the incident room. I said I was no crank, I explained I was a spiritual medium and usually what I got was correct, Spirit wouldn't muck about. I explained everything that I had seen and felt, to the airfield, the car and the three-syllable name, but I also said there were two people, possibly three involved plus the two girls. Well, I was thanked for my information and told they would make a note of it. Could they get back to me? My answer was, "I have nothing to hide but I do not want publicity."

I never heard again from the police but a week later it was announced on the news and the television that the youngsters had been found, in the spot I had seen, rather badly knocked about. I felt mutilated. They had discovered the girls not far from the fence I had seen, near the airport, and a car involved was the car that I had seen, and so was the three-syllable name. This is a part of mediumship, which is not nice, because what it does to you is unbelievable. In many ways mediumship is a gift, a special gift, but sometimes it can break your heart.

PEACE COMES

Any medium will tell you that a private sitting takes more energy and very often leaves the medium feeling very tired. It is said that we protect ourselves, and yes we do. It is also said that we feel the presence of people and their symptoms but there are times when I, like most, let my guard down and I get too involved. I sometimes find I have to be very strong and hold back my tears, for some sittings are very emotional. Though whatever you do in any way of life or whatever you are, you are human and a heart is human.

One particular sitting I had was with quite a young lady. I knew nothing about her, as we had preferred it to be that way when she arrived. She came in and sat down and I could feel the utter, utter pain within her. I could feel her loneliness and I knew for a fact that she had been desperately thinking of joining the Spirit loved ones. Who are we to judge? We are not. As the sitting started I was very much aware of a young gentleman, about 5ft 8in, big built, with plenty of meat on his bones, there was no doubt, and a mop of black wavy hair. He said to me his wife was very embarrassed about coming and I thought, why should she be embarrassed? Then he started to laugh. It was what I would term as a belly laugh, and as I looked at him I thought he must have been a joy to his good lady.

He started to tell her of things about their personal way of life, things that only she knew and then again he started to laugh. He said, "You know I wasn't ill, why, I was on top of the world, I was in good form, you'd have thought so anyway." He went on, "I can tell you this, I died with a smile on my face, I died doing what I liked most." I looked at him, again the laughter was coming and he proceeded to tell me that he had died 'on the job' as he called it. And I thought, 'on the job', working? No, and then of course it became clear, he had died in his own bed doing what he liked most.

This is what my sitter was embarrassed about. I said, "You don't have to worry, I have heard stranger things than that. He's quite happy to tell you what better way to meet God than with a smile on your face, and in the company of the best person you love." And to my amazement she looked at me and she said, "I have kept this a secret from all I can, I was embarrassed to admit what happened, I was mortified for people to know how he died, so I just said he died beside me to some people," she said, "but if he's not embarrassed, why should I be?" And to this I replied, "His proof of survival is that he was a happy fellow and he was happy the way he went over, even though the shock for you has been hard to bear."

He then started to tell her about the bedroom. He described the bedroom rail in the wardrobe; saying it had fallen down two nights before, which she confirmed. Then he started to talk to her about the window latch that was broken, and he advised her to get it repaired quickly. She smiled again, "Completely right," she said, "he doesn't miss a thing." And then he turned and said to her, "Let's get the insurance settled," and at this my mind took over and I thought he meant funeral insurance or likewise, but he shook his head. "No, it's the damn car. She's got to insure the car in just one name, save herself a few bob." I explained this to her and she answered, "I looked at the papers this morning but couldn't bring myself to do anything about it. Now I know I've got to and I know now that he's all right, and he must know how much I loved him." To this he shouted in reply, "Woman, maybe I never told you a lot," he said, "but I worshipped the ground you walked on!" When I relayed all this to her the tears were streaming down her face and she said, "I will sleep tonight for the first time since his passing, and thank you."

WHEN IT'S TIME TO GO

Two years ago I was in hospital, I wasn't good at all. I was in intensive care and I felt ill, really ill. I lay there, and as even when I'm ill I'm a fidget, I kept on moving and the machines would go off. I think in the end they got a bit fed up with me, but never mind. As I lay there during the night a gentleman appeared at the bottom of my bed. He smiled at me and my reaction was, "Blimey, somebody's come for me, but I'm not going yet, I've got things to do."

He smiled, walked straight past me and moved to the next bed. As he looked at me I thought, this man is on his mission, he's come to fetch somebody, there's no doubt about that but he doesn't belong to me. He moved two beds up the ward and stood at the end of the bed. I felt the glow of Spirit all around him and I felt the enlightenment of love. Then I heard a sigh from the bed, it was from a lady who had been fighting hard for her life. Suddenly the machines went off and there were nurses everywhere and the next thing, yes, the curtains were drawn around her bed and Spirits had claimed their own.

And let me tell this to you, my friends, never ever do you walk into the Spirit world alone. There is always someone there for you, usually someone who has loved you, loved you on the earth plane and loves you in the Spirit world. If not, there is always someone also who is allotted to you, to care and to ease your path. They may come as you remember, as an older version, they may come as a younger version, but you will know them and this I promise you, you will know the love that they hold out to you for I have witnessed that and you will never walk into the other world on your own. You are escorted with love and you are then again reunited with people you love, have loved or who love you, and you will never be lonely.

GONE

When I am gone, think not sad thoughts of me,
Remember all the fun we shared you and I
The fun, the joy, all the good times gone by
This is the way to remember me
Remember the laughs over silly things
Remember the smiles. Be glad what we had,
Friendship that you and I shared will never die.
The bond that held us close
Will never fade, neither will it go.
This dear friend, I tell you so.
Nothing can ever take the memories away.
Death is only a moving on,
To prepare for a better way,
Again we will laugh together and share our thoughts of days gone.

MY THOUGHTS ON THE SPIRITUAL PATH

Some mediums leave a little of their knowledge behind them, perhaps in actions or spoken thoughts. This is the same for anyone who lives their earthly life, proof of survival is mediumship.

Any fool can fill a client's head with a load of nonsense saying, "Oh yes, you are going to meet someone special, a love of your life, or you are going to come into money." Again, codswallop, that is supposed to be fortune-telling. This is not responsible behaviour and neither do those types of words hold credibility. That is not spiritual and has no proof of survival. Mediumship is the knowledge that your communicator is of Spirit, and that the information is from a reputable source.

I myself know that without a doubt there is a life beyond death and there is nothing more comforting than to be able to say to someone, yes, he or she is alive in a different dimension, there is life after death.

There is no death, just the leaving behind of a shell and stepping away from pain and discomfort.

I lost the sight of my right eye when I was four, through measles followed by complications. After many painful treatments and examinations it was decided to remove the eye and I would be furbished with another eye. Contrary to what people think now of me, I am still very self-conscious and hate looking straight at anyone's face.

During the later years of mediumship when we talk about the Third Eye, let me point this out: I have many Third Eyes – in colours of my choosing. I should point out that when I work as a medium mystically I have a red mark in the middle of my forehead, which seems very obvious during my work – certainly not an extra brain!

The medium's life is not always easy. We have to tread a road of understanding to enable us to understand others and the problems of life.

PROTECTION FOR ALL

In many ways mediums can be hurt in the emotional state. There are times in our lives when sensitivity is not always a boon. It is so easy for a sensitive to pick up on another's mood and sadness and unless one fully understands the meaning of protection a medium can feel drained of energy, and so very tired and physically exhausted this way. This is why we say, please learn to close down, and use this exercise regularly. I always think that this technique is not known to enough people, and that people are not furnished with the facts and knowledge on this very important point. The closing procedure is most important, this I stress time and time again. I find it very difficult to visualise what other mediums use as their closing down routines.

I use a system which I can visualise with ease.

I imagine a straightforward lid. I bring this lid over my crown chakra, which represents to me a very strong source of awareness. I visualise violet in colour.

Then we proceed to the Third Eye (brow). This gives spiritual insight, intuition and psychic perception, and from this comes the opening to a higher level, colour indigo.

Throat Chakra – Blue
A direction to a higher level, this chakra opens spiritual contact and is to me a very important part of the higher self.

Heart Chakra – Green
Heart gives the ability to care, and needs to be balanced with personal issues.

Solar Plexus Chakra – Yellow
Emotions are felt very strongly from this area; there is a very strong astral connection, which brings vulnerability and needs careful understanding. This chakra is a major physical point and emotions are felt here. Clairvoyance also is a key factor of this chakra.

Sacral Base Chakra – Orange
This is an area that holds healing energy at personal and non-personal level.

Private Area – Red
This applies to and speaks of strong energy, and sets steadfast the foundations in grounding and security of work.

HOW TO CENTRE OR GROUND YOURSELF – SUGGESTIONS

Centring oneself needs to be done on both a physical and a conscious 'being' level. First, be aware of the centre of your physical being by focussing on a line down the centre of yourself and feeling the air going down into your lungs.

Next, become conscious of a deep stillness within, allowing outer distractions to subside. The words, "Be still and know that I am God," are helpful with the realisation that at our core we are each a spark of God, or just the words, "Be still".

Imagine your breath streaming up and down through your body, gradually extending it down into the earth and up into the cosmos as you breathe in and out, thus connecting with both cosmic and gravitational energies.

Visualise roots growing down into the earth from the soles of your feet.

MYSELF ON CLOSING

I, at the end of the day, spend the proverbial penny. I make sure I put my feet firmly on the ground. Then I visualise a white light through my body. Next I wrap myself in a spiral of light. Then I place myself in a pyramid and I strongly say, "Anything that is not of God I do not want, I will not accept, and most important, I thank my friends of Spirit for being with me and thank them for their time and help."

This may sound weird to some people, yet colours play a big part in my life. If I feel I need extra energy I go for a red colour. Yet I find for my working-dress I love the spiritual mauves, the blue that speaks of healing and the yellow of spiritual thoughts. I try not to wear black as I find it very severe and I am not an austere person. I know I should wear black because it is very slimming in appearance and is more flattering to my ample proportions. Tough cheese! As long as I have a smile on my face, perhaps the audience won't worry too much about the bumps and baggage around my waist.

As I have said, no two mediums work the same and no two sittings are the same. Every medium has his or her own style, and this is what makes individuality.

The greatest responsibility of a medium is to treat with care other people's feelings. Compassion is one of the priorities, as is remembering that a single word can bring untold grief to someone. By the same token, during a sitting it is very easy to hear something and decide not to give it because it seems nonsense to you, yet very often it is the whole proof of a survival link.

I get very cross when unprincipled mediums hurt and destroy memories. One such occasion was when, in the middle of the night, I was called to a friend's hotel. There he had a guest who had been to a certain medium, who had charged this poor man the earth in money, and he was feeling very suicidal. The so-called medium had told the client that his wife had taken her own life because she did not want to return home. The gentleman was distraught, so I sat with him and we started to talk.

As soon as I opened my mouth his lovely wife was there. She had a very strange name, she was a German Jew, and then she showed me the numbers on her arm very clearly. To this my client confirmed the numbers at a later date. She started to tell him of being so upset about him and said in no uncertain terms that he knew the facts and what he had previously been told was untrue. She then asked me to ask him about the words on their wedding ring and she told me what was engraved inside the ring, it was, 'forever mine, forever thine.' Again, the gentleman started to cry, broken-hearted, he needed to get his emotions out. Then she told me what had happened and I related it back to the husband. It was the day she died, she was all ready to go home and was just waiting to be collected when she dropped dead without any warning just as he got to the hospital.

No wonder he was distraught on hearing all the nonsense the other so-called medium had said. It is the likes of those people who bring disrepute to honest mediums.

It was time for me to go and my new friend held out his wallet, asking, "Whatever you charge it will never be enough for the piece of mind you have given me." My answer was that I hoped I had righted a wrong, by which another had brought into disrepute the Code of Practice.

This is the true medium's aim, knowing that there is a life beyond death, and a future for those who wish to meet again.

LIVE EACH DAY

As mediums we know that people leave their impact upon the world in which they have lived. If they can say to other people, "I know", it gives the conviction of words but it does not always give the strong knowledge to others. It is easy to say, "I have seen, I have heard, I have known," but it is harder for other people to say, "Yes, we believe, we understand, we know." Through your stages of life as a medium you must always know that proof of survival gives mediumship. Any fool can say, "Oh yes, you are going to meet somebody special etc." That is what the sitter wants, but it is not what the Spirit wants.

The Spirit needs to say that there is a life beyond death, that there isn't a death, just a leaving behind of a shell of a body, which the soul leaves behind; and once a body has decayed and its earthly state has finished, the soul moves away. If some people say at the time of passing, "I will be afraid, I will fight it," then is time for the assurance of others to say, "You won't, you will be all right." It's a stepping stone from one life to the next. It's the easiest step you will ever take and it is the most unique. Every day of our lives we walk a path, a path that says, could I have done it this way? Could I have perhaps helped someone else? Could I have shared joy and not given tears? And no one can honestly say, "Everything I did is right, I know what I am." Yes, you know what you are but are you what you were meant to be? No one is. So when you enter the spiritual plane many of us call Heaven, then it will be your time to look back upon yourself and look back upon yourself as you have been as a person. Self-judgment is for all.

Our God does not judge us with an iron rod, or with a belt so strong that it could break your back. But we judge ourselves according to our lives and if we are truthful as we will have to be, then we will say to ourselves, "I could have done this, I wasn't hard enough on myself. I did not do this, I should have done otherwise, or I should not have said those words, I should have said more." Imagine. You will judge yourself on a higher level with intensity and honesty. Whereas you could not be honest on earth, you will be honest with yourself above.

Life is for learning. Life is being ready to progress into another state and this is what you will do. Reassured, everyone has this plan and it is best to equip ourselves on the earth plane to know the future plan so that when the time is right for you to enter into a higher state, you will be ready. There will be no turning round and saying, "I will come back tomorrow," for every life has a plan, every footstep has a road to tread and when you have finished your plan, whether you have done it well or indifferently, then you go. So I say to you my friends, live each day as it comes for it comes with goodness. Live each hour in order to progress. Let the regrets go but knowledge come forth, and in all things be true to yourself, be true to your knowledge of a higher life and seek the answers from within.

The soul very often cries, "Help me!" Our God helps us. Our Spirit friends help us. The body says, "Leave me," and at the time of our parting from this life, we leave the body. The body is of no use to us, it's just a shell, a cloak to wrap the bones in, a cloak to wrap the equipment we have used on the earth plane; we need it not so we cast off this body and go forward. The Spirit moves on and the soul rejoices for this is the beginning of another phase of life and again, I say to you, there is no death, only life; there is no death, only love, and love will reign. If your heart has cried on the earth plane for someone who has gone ahead, be assured they will still be within your reach on the other side. Their smile will welcome you and their love will touch your heart and your heart will rejoice. Your body will be whole. There will be nothing lacking, nothing gained, that should not be there, and in all things you will be the original child of grace, child of God, child of love and yourself, a spirit kindled by new life.

We ask ourselves, what is an angel? We ask ourselves why? Why me?

All these questions we ask when we are in trouble and I say to you, my angel holds my soul when I am praying. My angel touches my heart when I need to love. My angel comforts me when I am sad. My angel dries my tears when I cry and when I need the love of the Spirit, when I need the love of others, I call to my angel, "Please help me." Do not be afraid to call upon your angel for they always come, they will always be there.

Feel the love hold you, feel the truth around you. Who is your angel? Your angel is love, your angel is joy and your angel is a messenger of God. When you are afraid, remember you are never alone. Also remember, we all fear at sometime in our lives. We must remember that whatever we do in life, people have passed this path of life before. They have known the pitfalls. We are not unique, we are human. The only thing that we need to know is that God lives forever, God is light, God is love, God is within, your only need, and you are the child of one God.

Every leaf has a pattern. Every leaf has a purpose. And as a falling leaf comes to the ground, it is time to reflect. The leaves show you a line of life. The life you have is reflected in all you do and all you say. When you listen to your heart, do you hear the truth within you? When you listen to your soul, do you hear the soul speaking or the mind of all these things? Life has purpose and the purpose of living is to know; to know your path that you wish to tread, to know the soul that lives within the body. And the soul that escapes the body on passing is unique because it is the way to run. It can run to the heavens above and seek the love of God but sometimes the earthly soul in torment cries, "Help me!"

When this happens, rest assured, if it is asked of others to help with truth, then it will be answered. Do not be afraid to speak your heart and do not be afraid to speak your mind but be afraid of what you hear. For sometimes the heart will talk of things private and personal, and you will hear what you wish to hear. If you were honest, think, is this the heart speaking? Is this the mind speaking? Is this the soul? Is this the Spirit? And if you can answer these things in truth, then you are a wise one.

It is not always easy to differentiate between the stages of man. Man's life starts as an embryo on the earth plane but the life given is part of a pre-determined plan. For every being has its own perfection. Every limb of a human or an animal has its own form and says many things. It talks of family, it talks of ancestors, and of many different ways of the world. One looks at a fox and one sees the eyes of a fox, bright, clear and sparkling. Its ears are there to help it to adapt to its way of life. On a cold winter's day the coat of the fox protects the bones and the body and that which is within.

The human is also like that, we have two legs to walk, to run, to jump, two legs to carry us for our daily chores. We have two arms to hold, to embrace, to nurse a baby when needed, to lift a load when asked and to give thoughts in mind and body language to others. Of all these things everything has a purpose, everything has a way to run and this is life. When the body decays, whether man, beast, animal of any type, it is time for that earthly body to go back into a different dimension. The body rots and returns to mother earth to replenish other living things, another day, but rest assured, from all these things the soul moves on.

The soul is the part that says, "I have learnt, I have known, I am," and the Spirit says, "I will teach, I will instruct, I will prove who I am and of all things all must come to one. When your life span is finished and your days have long gone, remember this, your road was set for a purpose. Whoever you touched on your road of life you leave a little of yourself behind with them, wherever you go on your road of life, you leave something behind. When your road is hard, tread carefully, and when the road is slippery, take care, and when you have fear within you, do not be afraid to ask for help, do not be afraid to say, "I need to be loved, I need care, I am me." Never be afraid to say, "I need, I love, I am."

Of all your life's span there will come a time when you will reflect on what you have done with your life, and if you can answer honestly and say to yourself, and say to your Maker, "I have done the best I can, I have used the gifts you have given me and I have hopefully used them well," then you will be satisfied. But at all times in everyone's life very few people can say, "I am what I was supposed to be," and so, as each day of your journey progresses and each morning of your life awakens, look for a road that says fulfilment, look for a road to help others because a helping hand will help others, can help yourself. How can you know when someone cries and cries alone? Watch, listen, think and say to yourself, "That could be me, that could be me crying for help, please let me help them, please let me see," and in asking this for others you ask for yourself, and you ask for the inner child to know its God and to know its purpose, its Maker, its soul and the beginning. And the beginning is the end and the end is the beginning.

OLDER AND WISER

This is my 66th year and I am a lot wiser and in fact a lot wider. I am still a scatterbrain, and very much feeling my age with nine grandchildren and two great-granddaughters. I love them dearly, every one of them. I am never surprised at anything that happens to me, as I believe nothing happens by chance. Whoever we meet, wherever we go, it is part of a plan, not always to our understanding, but a pattern of life. When I went to the world of Spirit at the age of 32, I realised every day was special. At that time my aim was to see my sons grow up. Then the added bonus came when they were men and met their own future partners. Now I have a double bonus of grandchildren and great-grandchildren. I can work in the way I believe Spirit meant of me. Perhaps I can show someone else through my work the future life.

Spirits never ever surprise me and the love they bring to me and guidance and fulfilment is a joy I hope I am worthy of. At last I can do the work they intended of me when they gave me extra years. My main wish is to do them justice and my ever grateful thanks to my guides, my helpers, those who channelled me and of course my family; a very patient husband who sometimes must think I am a nutcase, and not forgetting my very special friends who also make my life easier. I know as long as there is work for me to do for Spirit I will do it. Only God on high will say when they are ready and then like everyone else I will not be able to argue. I will not say, just five more minutes, I will have to go, and I give thanks to God for the life he has given me and the work he has given me the privilege to do.

I am a very ordinary person living a very colourful life, now travelling abroad and at home around the churches, hopefully proving to the best of my ability, proof of survival. I would like time to complete what I wish to do and hope that it will be so and again I say; only God knows.

MARGARET HURDMAN

I am 66 years of age and still working for Spirit. Most of my life was spent in the Midlands and then I moved to Llandudno, North Wales, where I have been for twenty-four years. I am just an ordinary person and through illness in my life I have been given a gift in later years to give proof of survival in the next world.

It may seem strange that a great-grandmother is starting life again. In the last six years, I can honestly say, that there is a need for people all over the world to have the comfort of knowing that there is life after death. Thanks to enlightenment, to television and radio, more people are receiving the word. Everywhere I go is a special place to work. There are many tours planned for the future all over the world. That is my reason for being given the second chance to live; only God knows when he wishes me to go back. God is the boss, I am only a vessel. There is a lot still to be told of happenings and experience. I pray that time will allow me to share my thoughts and a future long enough to tell you more.

Cover Design: S. Fairgrieve

Layout: S. Fairgrieve

Font: Adobe Garamond (11pt)

Copies of this book can be ordered via the Internet:

                   www.librario.com

or from:

                   Librario Publishing Ltd
                   Brough House
                   Milton Brodie
                   Kinloss
                   Moray IV36 2UA
                   Tel / Fax No 01343 850 617